ஐ OPPOSITIONS IN CHAUCER

BY PETER ELBOW

WESLEYAN UNIVERSITY

PRESS ஐ MIDDLETOWN

CONNECTICUT

The publisher gratefully acknowledges the support of the publication of this book by The Andrew W. Mellon Foundation.

An earlier version of the chapter on *Troilus and Criseyde* appeared in *Literary Criticism and Historical Understanding: English Institute Essays,* a collection edited by Philip Damon and published by Columbia University Press in 1967; and a slightly different version of the chapter on *The Knight's Tale* was published in *Chaucer Review* in 1973.

Library of Congress Cataloging in Publication Data

Elbow, Peter, 1935–
    Oppositions in Chaucer.

    Includes bibliographical references.
    1. Chaucer, Geoffrey, d. 1400 — Technique. 2. Irony in literature. 3. Boethius, d. 524 — De consolatione philosophiae. I. Title.
PR1924.E45   821'.1   75–16216
ISBN 0–8195–4087–0

Manufactured in the United States of America

First edition

TO MY MOTHER AND MY FATHER

CONTENTS

OPPOSITIONS IN CHAUCER

It may perhaps be that nature has a liking for con-traries and evolves harmony out of them and not out of similarities. . . . The arts . . . apparently imitate nature in this respect. — ARISTOTLE

In formal logic, a contradiction is the sign of a defeat; but in the evolution of real knowledge, it marks the first step in progress toward a victory.

— ALFRED NORTH WHITEHEAD

The opposite of a correct statement is a false state-ment. But the opposite of a profound truth may well be another profound truth. — NIELS BOHR

No mind can engender until divided into two.

— WILLIAM BUTLER YEATS

The chief characteristic of the mind is to be con-stantly describing itself. — HENRI FOCILLON

INTRODUCTION

This is a study that explores a particular pattern of thinking in Boethius and Chaucer and tries to show why it is important. My contention is that both men have an ingrained tendency to see oppositions everywhere, but to deal with them in such a way that both sides remain affirmed.

In Chapter 1 I show how *The Consolation of Philosophy* is organized in terms of this pattern of thinking which Boethius himself pointedly describes:

"But now let us set our arguments against each other and perhaps from their opposition some special truth will emerge." (III, Pr. 12)

"What God has set such conflict between these two truths? Separately each is certain, but put together they cannot be reconciled. Is there no discord between them? Can they exist side by side and be equally true?" (v, Met. 3)[1]

Chaucer's *Troilus and Criseyde, The Knight's Tale,* and *The Nun's Priest's Tale* are each constructed in terms of a polar opposition: in *Troilus and Criseyde* whether two philosophical speeches are true or false; in *The Knight's Tale* whether Palamon or Arcite is more worthy of Emelye; in *The Nun's Priest's Tale* whether Chauntecleer's dream is prophetic or mean-

ingless. In each poem Chaucer affirms both sides
equally. In Chapters II, III, and IV I describe how he ac-
complishes this double affirmation and how he uses
a different method in each case. In Chapter V I describe how Chaucer transcends the opposition between freedom and necessity at many different places
in his poetry — often even when he seems to be dealing
with something entirely different.

But at certain crucial points, especially at major
endings, Chaucer relinquishes this dialectic and in
fact chooses one side as right and rejects the other as
wrong. In Chapter VI I describe how and why Chaucer
does so, and I compare him to the Pardoner, a character whom he endows with his own capacity for complex irony, but not with his capacity for relinquishing
it.

I do not assert that Chaucer uses this pattern at
all times. I explore only some of his poetry, though
some of the most important. But I do believe that this
dialectic is central to his technique. It is, for example, intimately related to the most striking quality in
Chaucer's style, his complex irony, which can be understood as a way of saying opposite things simultaneously without either being undermined by the other.
This book could be called a study in Chaucer's irony.

This book is not an historical study. In trying to
elucidate a pattern of thinking I refrain from trying
to say how Boethius and Chaucer came to have it.
Dichotomies have always appealed to the human
mind. A polar opposition can order the widest possible spectrum of otherwise chaotic phenomena. To

have the idea of freedom versus necessity is to have a handle for organizing *all* behavior. Up versus down takes care of almost everything. Aristotle made generation from contraries the cornerstone of his philosophy, and he was following a tradition from the preSocratics. A preoccupation with the interaction of opposites characterizes the basic thinking of many cultures, as in *Yin* and *Yang*,[2] for example.

Perhaps Chaucer learned this pattern from translating Boethius's *Consolation of Philosophy*. What better way to adopt a habit of thinking? But there are differences between the ways in which Boethius and Chaucer transcended opposites, and so I hesitate to say that that is what happened. In the medieval period more than in most other periods, thinkers took it for granted that conflicting and even contradictory ideas might both be true. It was a time when, presented with an opposition, one might be instinctively more interested in showing how both sides were true than how one of them was false.[3] There was Aquinas organizing his great work in terms of oppositions, though not refraining from choosing between them. There was Abelard making a book out of a list of opposites, *Sic et Non*. There was Nicholas of Cusa — though he lived after Chaucer — believing that one perceives reality truly only by rising above reason and the principle of noncontradiction to affirm contradictory statements. Among rhetorical "figures of thought" taught to help one find and organize material, there were those that involved antithesis and reconciliation of opposites — *contentio* and *concordia discors*. But I avail myself of another, *occupatio,* and leave it to others, more learned and brave, to speak of historical or personal influence.

I cannot resist, however, speculating in the final chapter on some of the reasons why this kind of thinking seems so important, so fertile and profound: how it can make persons wiser by helping them to overcome the limitations of perception, language, and the single human point of view. In occasionally using the word *dialectic* for this pattern of thinking I do not mean to stress the full Hegelian process that ends up with a complete new synthesis so much as the seminal process of understanding a subject in terms of opposites and seeing both sides as right.

In my reading of Chaucer, though I did not set out to do so, I end up following a lead suggested by some of Chaucer's best readers. Talbot Donaldson's continued exploration of Chaucer's irony and use of personae points to my study:

. . . the poet arranges for the moralist to define austerely what ought to be and for his fictional representative . . . to go on affirming affectionately what is. The two points of view, in strict moral logic diametrically opposed, are somehow made harmonious in Chaucer's wonderfully comic attitude, that double vision that is his ironical essence.[4]

Charles Muscatine, Dorothy Everett, Robert Payne, and Ida Gordon make similar observations about the centrality of Chaucer's double vision or complex irony.[5] I am particularly indebted to the work of these scholars and others in more ways than could possibly be acknowledged in footnotes. And I have tried to use few footnotes.

Donaldson concludes *Chaucer the Pilgrim* by saying that it is often impossible to know which of two opposed voices has the last word. In essence, mine is a study that tries to show *how* Chaucer could succeed in saying opposite things at the same time and have them both remain said, and also *why* it is valuable to do so. I have tried to write a work useful to both specialists and general readers, whether they are interested in Chaucer or interested in the relationship between literature and structures of thinking. Readers with no interest at all in Boethius may skip Chapter I and still follow easily the succeeding chapters about Chaucer.

In my lack of historical emphasis, I may have done what the historical scholar D. W. Robertson was trying to warn against when he wrote that "the medieval world with its quiet hierarchies . . . was innocent of our profound concern for tension. . . . It was a world without dynamically interacting polarities."[6] Robertson demonstrates that his judgment fits medieval religious and aesthetic *theory,* but I do not think that he demonstrates that it fits the poetic practice of a writer like Chaucer. Nevertheless, Robertson rightly warns against reading medieval literature as though it were modern poetry. What follows is not a study of how paradox-laden imagery produces strong emotional tension, though emotional tension is not absent from Chaucer's poetry as Robertson implies. Rather, it is a study of how a particular pattern of thinking helped Chaucer quietly to increase the amount of truth he saw and communicated.

When I was discouraged about ever finding a publisher, Talbot Donaldson's encouragement kept me trying. I am all the more grateful because I did not have any claim on his time or attention. I wish also to express deep gratitude to those who read my manuscript and gave helpful suggestions or criticism: Murray Biggs, Charles Blythe, Thad Curtz, J. V. Cunningham, Allan Grossman, Judith Grossman, A. R. Gurney, Jr., Karen Klein, Roy Lamson, Rose Moss, and students in a Chaucer seminar at Evergreen State College. And I want particularly to thank John Hackett and Donald Howard for their comments. I do not intend, however, to implicate any of these people in positions or shortcomings that are altogether my own.

Joan Hopper and Carmela Ortigas helped me with excellent typing.

This book could not have been written without the help and support given me by my wife Cami, and it has benefited immensely from her editorial counsel.

PETER ELBOW

August, 1975
Olympia, Washington

I. BOETHIUS'
THE CONSOLATION OF
PHILOSOPHY

BOETHIUS[7] lived in the midst of oppositions. Rome, at the end of the fifth century A.D. and the beginning of the sixth, was the site of the overlapping between the cultures of Rome and the invading Germanic conquerors, between the Roman Western and the Hellenic Eastern empires, between the ancient and the modern eras, and above all, between Christian and pagan thought — not to mention conflicts between various Christian sects. Perhaps it was this setting that gave Boethius his instinct to transcend oppositions.

As a young man, he decided to translate and comment on all the works of Plato and Aristotle in order to demonstrate a harmony between their contrasting positions.[8] To set out on such a huge task early in his life showed his temperamental bent. It must have been an *a priori* urge to transcend what are the two paradigmatic opposite ways of thinking about things since he could not have had it all worked out in advance. Throughout his life Boethius was a scholar — translator, commentator, and philosopher. He was a major influence on scholars and philosophers for more than a thousand years, and his *Consolation* was one of the most influential and widely read books throughout all of the Middle Ages and the Renaissance. But Boethius was also drawn in the opposite direction. He felt that the philosopher should concern himself with government. He was a consul early in his life, and at the time of his downfall he held one of the highest offices in the Roman government of the Western Empire. Boethius worked on reconciling doctrinal differences between the Western and Eastern churches, but he was accused of espionage to bring *political* union between the Eastern and Western empires.

There were other charges as well.[9] He was exiled, imprisoned, tortured, and finally put to death. He wrote the *Consolation* in prison, awaiting execution, in an attempt to come to grips with what had happened to him and to deal with his despair. The book, like his life, represents a bridging of theory and practice. It is both a vehicle for purely abstract moral philosophy and an autobiography in which he deals with the details of his personal life and his feelings. It also represents, through its alternation of prose and poetry, a reconciling of abstract philosophic argument and poetic vision.

But above all it is a transcending of the opposition that Boethius seemed most intent on bridging throughout his life, that between Christian and pagan. The *Consolation* is a work of moral philosophy, and even of theology, but in it Boethius restricts himself to the use of natural reason and philosophy. He leaves out all traces of Christian revelation. Yet he reaches conclusions completely in harmony with those of the early fathers of the Church.[10] Commentators from the ninth century to the present argue whether the book is Christian or pagan.[11] It is both. Repeatedly Boethius transcends distinctions that were usually sharpened as a way of dividing Christian from pagan. For example, there is the question of whether the world is fallen or good. Boethius answers that it is both.[12] To the question of whether the universe is eternal or not — another touchstone for Christianity — Boethius answers that it is neither: it has no beginning or end, yet it is not eternal (out of time) as God is; it is "perpetual."[13] To the question of whether events are subject to blind Fate or to divine Providence, he answers that they are subject to both:

"Thus Providence is the unfolding of temporal events as this is present to the vision of the divine mind; but this same unfolding of events as it is worked out in time is called Fate." (IV, Pr. 6)[14]

To the question of whether human actions are subject to free will or to divine foreknowledge, he answers, in the fifth book of the *Consolation,* that they are subject to both.

In the rest of this chapter I shall explore in more detail the metaphorical and dialectical strategies for transcending key oppositions that Boethius used in the *Consolation.*

When someone is in prison awaiting execution, he brings great authority to the philosophical question at the heart of the *Consolation,* the question of freedom and necessity. The *Consolation* is a dialogue in which Boethius is instructed Socratically by the figure of Dame Philosophy, who appears to Boethius in a vision at the start. The book moves from the feeling of constraint to the feeling of freedom. Boethius, in the voice of Dame Philosophy, talks himself, as it were, out of jail.

The first four books of the *Consolation* concentrate on necessity; Book v focuses on freedom. Its first question is why God does not put human behavior under the control of divine necessity:

"You govern all things, each according to its destined purpose. Human acts alone, O Ruler of All, You refuse to restrain within just bounds. Why should uncertain Fortune control our lives?" (i, Met. 5)

Books i through iv are required before Boethius understands and is convinced by Dame Philosophy that divine necessity does indeed rule all human actions. Sometimes after he is led through a long demonstration, he returns all over again to another version of the same question. As late as Book iv he asks, "Here, though, is the greatest cause of my sadness: since there is a good governor of all things, how can there be evil, and how can it go unpunished?" (iv, Pr. 1). It is not until Book v that he seems sufficiently convinced of divine necessity to ask the opposite question: "But within this series of connected causes, does our will have any freedom, or are the motions of human souls also bound by the fatal chain?" (v, Pr. 2). And here in Book v the answer is that free will does prevail.

It is odd that where Boethius so often brings together the two elements of a dichotomy and explicitly cuts through the opposition (*e. g.,* the world as fallen/good; eternal/finite; Fate/Providence; foreknowledge/free will), he does not do this with freedom and necessity. In fact it seems at first as though Book v's affirmation of free will *contradicts* the earlier books' affirmation of divine necessity: that is, even though Book v preserves human will from God's *foreknowing,* it does not preserve it from God's *foreplanning* or *governing.* The argument for free will in Book v could apply to a God who just sat back and observed events over which He had no control. (The word *providence* contains ambiguously the two notions *foreknowing* and *foreplanning.*)

But Boethius prevents this seeming contradiction. His argument for necessity in Books I–IV — the argument for God's foreplanning or governing — does *not* compromise free will as argued in Book v. God does not govern human events by an active or controlling intervention. He does not meddle. He governs, rather, through having structured things so that free human actions conform to divine law. God structured man and the universe in relation to each other so that real human happiness comes only from pursuing the good. Men who pursue the good have the only imperishable happiness. They are in fact happy even if they appear unsuccessful. But men who turn away from the good, or who seek only a portion of the good, such as money, power, or fame, are not really happy even if they appear successful. Justice rules, thus, through the nature of things, and injustice is only an illusion. Human actions as well as natural phenomena conform to divine necessity. God rules not by intervention but by structure:

"Oh God, Maker of heaven and earth, Who govern the world with eternal reason, at your command time passes from the beginning. You place all things in motion, though You are yourself without change. No external causes impelled You to make this work from chaotic matter. *Rather it was the form of the highest good, existing within You without envy, which caused You to fashion all things according to the eternal exemplar.* You who are most beautiful produce the beautiful world from your divine mind and, forming it in your image, You order the perfect parts in a perfect whole." (III, Met. 9; emphasis added)[15]

In describing a nonintervening divine necessity, which does not compromise freedom, Boethius is implicitly using the Aristotelian concept of the unmoved mover. God or the good is the cause of everything, not by getting behind and pushing, but rather simply by *being* at the center of things, rewarding (through being) those things which turn toward the center and punishing (through privation) those which turn away. But though the Aristotelian term *unmoved mover* is not used, the Platonic concept of love rings very loud in the *Consolation*. Hymns and invocations to love-as-harmony are among the most powerful passages. Love-as-harmony is the way an unmoved mover gets things done — the principle of operation by which human actions can be at once free and in conformity to a higher plan:

"This is the common bond of love by which all things seek to be held to the goal of good. Only thus can things endure: drawn by love they turn again to the Cause which gave them being." (IV, Met. 6)

It is interesting that I must *argue* that divine law does not undermine human freedom in the *Consolation*. When Boethius talks of divine law in Books I–IV and human freedom in Book V, he does it in such a way that they do not conflict, but he does not bother to argue the point (as he does argue the coexistence of divine foreknowledge and human free will in Book V). It may be that we see here an historical phenomenon that Owen Barfield speaks of, especially in his essay "The Meaning of the Word 'Literal.' "[16] He argues that many of the concepts we think of as new metaphorical bridgings of opposites are really older than the elements that are bridged: people in earlier times could take the "metaphor" for granted but had to work to create what we feel as plain, literal distinctions. One of his examples is the Greek word *pneuma,* which we translate as either "breath" or "spirit." In Homer, when someone dies, the *pneuma* departs from him. Barfield argues that if you asked a Homeric contemporary which he meant, "breath" or "spirit" (however you might succeed in asking the question), he would not know what you meant. He would not feel the radical opposition between physical and spiritual that is so deeply imbedded in our language. The *creation* of such distinctions, the creation of much of what we think of as literal language, was a long slow job — one in which Socrates and Plato played a big role.

I do not mean to push Boethius too far back. He had fully digested the distinctions forged by Socrates, Plato, and Aristotle, and thus inhabited what is, in a sense, the modern universe of thought and language. But though Boethius is engaged in conscious, sophisticated argument for most of the *Consolation,* nevertheless in Books I–IV he seems to take for granted, or to find already there in his language, in concepts like 'love' and 'harmony,' that divine law does not compromise human freedom. It is not something he has to hammer out through argument. (What he is hammering out in argument in Books I–IV is that God's law *does* govern human action.)

If we look at Boethius' imagery, we see more clearly how he assumed a radical coexistence of freedom and necessity. For example, Dame Philosophy repeatedly uses the conventional figure of one's "native city" or one's "true country," but she characterizes it — without arguing the point at all — as a place where the citizen is at once perfectly free and also ruled by the laws of the one true king:

"You have not been driven out of your homeland; you have willfully wandered away. Or, if you prefer to think that you have been driven into exile, *you yourself have done the driving, since no one else could do it.* For if you can remember your true country you know that it is not, as

Athens once was, ruled by many persons; rather 'it has one ruler and one king,' who rejoices in the presence of citizens, not in their expulsion. To be governed by his power, and subject *to his laws is the greatest liberty.*" (I, Pr. 5; emphasis added)

In the second poem of Book III, Boethius uses imagery that intertwines freedom and necessity even more pointedly. The poem announces at the start that it will illustrate divine law and control. But it does so entirely with images of unchaining, uncaging, releasing:

"Now I will show you in graceful song, accompanied by pliant strings, how mighty Nature *guides the reins* of all things; how she providently *governs* the immense world by her *laws;* how she *controls* all things, *binding* them with unbreakable bonds.

"The Carthaginian lions endure their fair chains, are fed by hand, and fear the beatings they get from their masters; but if blood should smear their fierce mouths, their sluggish spirits revive, and with a roar they revert to their original nature. They *shake off their chains* and turn their mad fury on their masters, tearing them with bloody teeth.

"When the chattering bird, who sings in the high branches, is shut up in a narrow cage, she is not changed by the lavish care of the person who feeds her with sweet drink and tasty food. If she can *escape from the cramped cage* and see the cool shade of the wood, she will scatter the artificial food and *fly with yearning to the trees* where she will make the forest ring with her sweet voice.

"A treetop bent down by heavy pressure will bow its head to the ground; but if the pressure is released, the tree *looks back to heaven* again. Phoebus sets at night beneath the Hesperian waves, but returning again along his secret path he drives his chariot to the place where it always rises.

"Thus all things seek again their proper courses, and *rejoice when they return* to them. The only stable order in things is that which connects the beginning to the end and keeps itself on a steady course." (III, Met. 2; emphasis added)

One of the main messages of the *Consolation,* then — made through imagery as much as through argument — is that all events, even human actions, conform to divine law or necessity; yet freedom is unimpaired.

But if freedom is completely unimpaired by divine necessity, why are there so many references to extreme constraint or coercion? Hateful constraint is clearly one of Boethius' subjects. He is, after all, talking about prison. The clearest examples are images of slavery, exile, bondage, and tyranny:

"[Y]ou have submitted yourself to her chains . . . [y]ou have put yourself in Fortune's power." (II, Pr. 1)

"But, if the soul . . . is freed from this earthly prison . . ." (II, Pr. 7)

"But if you strip off the coverings of vain honor from those proud men, you will see underneath the *tight chains* they wear. Lust *rules* their hearts with greedy poisons, rage whips them, vexing their minds to stormy wrath. Sometimes they are slaves to sorrow, sometimes to delusive hope.

This is the picture of individual man with all his *tyrant* passions; *enslaved* by these evil powers, he *cannot do what he wishes*." (IV, Met. 2; emphasis added)

The fact is that Boethius implies two different ways in which freedom and necessity coexist. He implies — to use his geographical image — two regions. One is the region of one's "true city," where freedom and necessity coexist as just described. But when people leave (or forget) their true city, they enter a region where they are both free and bound in a *different* way: free because they put themselves there freely, and because (in the last analysis, at any rate) they can turn their eyes back to the light at any time; but bound, more tyrannically, by the chains of necessity. Thus the *Consolation* talks about *two* kinds of necessity: a free, unconstrained conformity to the higher law (providence) that comes from giving free rein to one's natural desire for true happiness (as in the case of the unfettered lion, bird, and tree); and a prisonlike constraint (fate) that comes from being turned around or not seeing things clearly. These two kinds of necessity can be clearly distinguished in the following passage:

"If . . . it is connected to the center, it is *confined by the simplicity of the center*. . . . [But] whatever strays farthest from the divine mind is most *entangled in the nets of Fate*." (IV, Pr. 6; emphasis added)

Just as persons in their true city have the "greatest liberty" in being "governed by [the] power and subject to [the] laws" of their "one ruler and one king," (I, Pr. 5), so those who leave their home "worsen the slavery to which they have brought themselves and are, as it were, the captives of their own freedom" (I, Pr. 5).

There is an opposition here which takes a number of forms in the *Consolation:* being an exile or being in one's own true city, being a slave or being a citizen, the good region or the bad region, prisonlike necessity or nonconstraining necessity, and the cave or the sky. I find this opposition between the cave and the sky, and the way Boethius finally transcends it, to be the imaginative center of the *Consolation.* First, I shall explore how this opposition pervades the whole work. Afterwards, I shall show how Boethius transcends it: that what looks like contradiction is really reconcilable.

The opposition between the cave and the sky is an implicit opposition between the two most famous and resonant epistemological metaphors from ancient times: slaves chained in Plato's cave, and the soul of Scipio Africanus looking down upon the tiny earth from the upper heavens (from Cicero's *De Republica,* made famous in Macrobius' *Somnium Scipionis*).[17]

The cave and sky images appear most fully and are contrasted most explicitly at the end of Book III and the start of Book IV. Book III ends with the story of Orpheus:

"Happy is he who can look into the shining spring of good; happy is he who can break the heavy chains of earth.

"Long ago the Thracian poet, Orpheus, mourned for his dead wife. With his sorrowful music he made the woodland dance and the rivers stand still. He made the fearful deer lie down bravely with the fierce lions; the rabbit no longer feared the dog quieted by his song.

"But as the sorrow within his breast burned more fiercely, that music which calmed all nature could not console its maker. Finding the gods unbending, he went to the regions of hell. There he sang sweet songs to the music of his harp, songs drawn from the noble fountains of his goddess mother, songs inspired by his powerless grief and the love which doubled his grief.

"Hell is moved to pity when, with his melodious prayer, he begs the favor of those shades. The three-headed guardian of the gate is paralyzed by that new song; and the Furies, avengers of crimes who torture guilty souls with fear, are touched and weep in pity. Ixion's head is not tormented by the swift wheel, and Tantalus, long maddened by his thirst, ignores the waters he now might drink. The vulture is filled by the melody and ignores the liver of Tityus.

"At last, the judge of souls, moved by pity, declares, 'We are conquered. We return to this man his wife, his companion, purchased by his song. But our gift is bound by the condition that he must not look back until he has left hell.' But who can give lovers a law? Love is a stronger law unto itself. As they approached the edge of night, Orpheus looked back at Eurydice, lost her, and died.

"This fable applies to all of you who seek to raise your minds to sovereign day. For whoever is conquered and turns his eyes to the pit of hell, looking into the inferno, loses all the excellence he has gained." (III, Met. 12)

Then Book IV answers this downward image by immediately turning upward ("raise your minds to sovereign day"):

"And since under my guidance you have understood the essence of true happiness, and have found out where it resides, I shall . . . show you the path which will take you home. And I shall give wings to your mind which can carry you aloft, so that, without further anxiety, you may return safely to your own country. . . .

"My wings are swift, able to soar beyond the heavens. The quick mind which wears them scorns the hateful earth and climbs above the globe of the immense sky, leaving the clouds below. It soars beyond the point of fire caused by the swift motion of the upper air until it reaches the house of stars. There it joins Phoebus in his path, or rides with the cold, old Saturn, companion of that flashing sphere, running along the starry circle where sparkling night is made. When it has seen enough, it flies beyond the farthest sphere to mount the top of the swift heaven and share the holy light.

"There the Lord of kings holds His scepter, governing the reins of the world. With sure control He drives the swift chariot, the shining judge of all things.

"If the road which you have forgotten, but now search for, brings you here, you will cry out: 'This I remember, this is my own country, here I was born and here I shall hold my place.' Then if you wish to look down upon the night of earthly things which you have left, you will see those much feared tyrants dwelling in exile here." (IV, Pr. 1, Met. 1)

The image of soaring in the sky brings together a whole set of related ideas from the work. This station aloft is man's "homeland" or his "own true city." It is the region of lightness, clear-sightedness; it gives a view of the heavens and detachment from concerns of the earth. Dame Philosophy's head touches the top of the heavens (I, Pr. 1). She says, "While they fight over things of no value, we laugh at them from above." (I, Pr. 3). And of course at the center of this figure are the connotations of freedom and release: though Dame Philosophy insists that human freedom is real however sunken one's condition, it is only when people take themselves aloft and stay in their own true city that this freedom is fully realized and *feels* free, unconstrained, and birdlike.

The image of the cave brings together a more diverse range of figures. Orpheus in hell parallels Boethius in prison. Both embody the essential implications of Plato's cave: both men are in a dark, heavily enclosed place, they are powerless, and they are "turned around," *i. e.,* they mourn and worry about what they should have the sense to put behind them. In addition, both are dominated and controlled by inconsolable grief, and both are musicians. In both cases, the power and expression of their grief are associated with poetry, music, and the muses — *i. e.,* with art. It is sweet grief, sweet beauty.

This sweetness of grief, beauty, and art is associated with poison, sickness, and wounds. For Orpheus, his sweet grief leads to death. Dame Philosophy calls herself a "physician" in her helping role, and "medicine" is the recurring metaphor for the curative rhetoric and dialectic she brings:

"If you want a doctor's help, you must uncover your wound." (I, Pr. 4)

"Who let these whores from the theater come to the bedside of this sick man?" she said. "They cannot offer medicine for his sorrows; they will nourish him only with their sweet poison. . . . they do not liberate the minds of men from disease. . . . Get out, you Sirens; your sweetness leads to death. Leave him to be cured and made strong by my Muses." (I, Pr. 1)

This dangerous sweetness is associated with jewels that came from caves deep in the earth:

"Nothing that the river Tagus with its golden shores can give, nor the Hermus with its jeweled banks, the Indus of the torrid zone, gleaming with green and white stones, none of these can clear man's vision. Instead, they hide blind souls in their shadows.

"Whatever pleases and excites your mind here, Earth has prepared in her deep caves. The shining light which rules and animates the heavens avoids the dark ruins of the soul. Whoever can see this light will discount even the bright rays of Phoebus." (III, Met. 10; emphasis added)

"Alas, what ignorance drives miserable men along crooked paths! You do not look for gold in the green trees, nor for jewels hanging on the vine; you do not set your nets in the high mountains when you want a fish for dinner; nor, if you want to hunt deer, do you seek them along the Tyrenean seas. On the contrary, men are skilled in knowing the hidden caves in the sea, and in knowing where white pearls and scarlet dye are found; they know what beaches are rich in various kinds of fish.

"But, when it comes to the location of the good which they desire, they are blind and ignorant. They dig the earth in search of the good which soars above the star-filled heavens." (III, Met. 8)

Boethius' and Orpheus' grief is associated with passivity and powerlessness. Boethius "lies here, bound down by heavy chains, the light of his mind gone out" (I, Met. 2). He is "suffering merely from lethargy" (I, Pr. 2). His writing of poetry is portrayed as passive rather than active: "Wounded Muses tell me what I must write" (I, Met. 1). "Once this man was free beneath the open heaven, and he used to run along heavenly paths" (I, Met. 2). Although Orpheus is not described as powerless, we are told that Orpheus' songs are inspired by his "powerless grief." Moreover, there is an association between him and powerlessness characteristic of dream displacement: his sweet music causes absolute powerlessness in everything else.

Grief and passivity are associated with fluidity — flowing water and turbulent winds. Powerlessness in a person comes from being overwhelmed by turbulent fluids. Tears, for example, "overpower" a person. The beauty of art expressing sadness is dangerous because, like tears, it wells up, overwhelms, drowns, and threatens him with its formlessness:

"You are so . . . blown about by the tumult of your feelings." (I, Pr. 5)

". . . elegiac verses bathe my face with real tears. . . . The sad hour . . . has nearly drowned me." (I, Met. 1)

"Alas! how this mind is dulled, drowned in the overwhelming depths. . . . Sick anxiety, inflated by worldly winds, swells his thoughts to bursting." (I, Met. 2)

"The serene man who has ordered his life stands above menacing fate and unflinchingly faces good and bad fortune. . . . The threatening and raging ocean storms which churn the waves cannot shake him; nor can the bursting furnace of Vesuvius, aimlessly throwing out its smoky fire." (I, Met. 4)

Orpheus' sweet songs, though less turbulent, are "drawn from the noble fountains of his goddess mother" (III, Met. 12).

The fluid turbulence which overwhelms one is, of course, feeling. And if one wants to regain agency and power over oneself, one must overpower feeling:

"He who hopes for nothing and fears nothing can disarm the fury of these impotent men; but he who is burdened by fears and desires is not master of himself . . . he fastens the chain by which he will be drawn." (I, Met. 4)

"If you want to see the truth in clear light . . . cast off all joy and fear. Fly from hope and sorrow. When these things rule, the mind is clouded and bound to the earth." (I, Met. 7)

The main thing about Orpheus and Boethius in prison is that they are overwhelmed by their feeings of grief.

Along with feelings, turbulence, and overwhelming fluids comes forgetfulness:

"In spite of its hazy memory, the human soul seeks to return to its true good; but, like the drunken man who cannot find his way home, the soul no longer knows what its good is." (III, Pr. 2)

"There is no danger. You are suffering merely from leth- argy, the common illness of deceived minds. You have for- gotten yourself a little, but you will quickly be yourself again. . . ." (I, Pr. 2)

"Now, I know another cause of your sickness, and the most important: you have forgotten what you are." (I, Pr. 6)

Here then is a rich opposition which subtly per- meates the book. On the one hand are images of dark- ness, blindness, being down in a cave deep in the earth, being in prison, being helpless, being over- whelmed by emotions in general and love-grief in particular; associated with all this are beauty, music, poetry, sweetness, fluids, turbulence, poison, sickness, passivity, and forgetfulness. On the other hand are images of soaring aloft at the top of the universe, out in the bright light or looking at the light, seeing all things clearly, unconstraining necessity or universal harmony, being unvexed by strong feelings or tur- bulence, smiling or laughing, and being self-suffi- cient; associated with all this are logic, dialectic, and truth. Above all, the cave is associated with complexity and multiplicity, the sky with simplicity and unity.[18] The following passage illustrates how this dichotomy of metaphoric connotations pervades Boethius' lan- guage:

"It is as if you were to look by turns at the sordid earth and at the heavens, compelled by the power of sight — and nothing else — to be now in the dirt, now among the stars.

Just because thoughtless men do not understand this, should we lower ourselves to those whom we have shown to be like beasts? If a man who had completely lost his sight should forget that he had ever been able to see, and be quite unaware of any natural disability, would we too think that this blind man could see?" (IV, Pr. 4)

Boethius reconciles this extended cave/sky opposition in a complex way. First of all, he bridges it with three concepts: love, woman, and music. Love rules both the cave and the sky. Love is the orderly force of harmony which emanates from God and Nature and is most often symbolized in the movement of the heavenly bodies:

"That the universe carries out its changing process in concord and with stable faith, that the conflicting seeds of things are held by everlasting law, that Phoebus in his golden chariot brings in the shining day, that the night, led by Hesperus, is ruled by Phoebe, that the greedy sea holds back his waves within lawful bounds, for they are not permitted to push back the unsettled earth — all this harmonious order of things is achieved by love which rules the earth and the seas, and commands the heavens." (II, Met. 8)

On the other hand, love is also that chaotic human attraction which wrests humans out of control of themselves and out of harmony with God and Nature:

"But who can give lovers a law? Love is a stronger law unto itself. As they approached the edge of night, Orpheus looked back at Eurydice, lost her, and died." (III, Met. 12)

The disruptive human love for lower things that destroys control is clearly associated with love for *woman:* the dark, tyrannical attraction of the cave. Yet the main voice for the higher love — the main voice for the whole *Consolation* — is that of a woman, Dame Philosophy. Her womanhood is neither trivial nor unnoticed. She takes a very motherly stance. And where the deception of the cave consists of sweet and turbulent fluids (winds, oceans, tears, even liquor in the case of the drunk man who does not know his home, and the "sweet poisons" of the whores of the theater), Dame Philosophy's truth is also fluid: "Are you not he who once was nourished by my milk?" (I, Pr. 2).

Boethius also associates *music* with both sides of the polarity. Sweet and powerful music (and poetry) characterizes Boethius in prison and Orpheus in hell. Yet of course it is the music and harmony of the universe that characterize the heavens.[19] In linking the cave and the sky through love, woman, and music, Boethius is building on the model Plato provided in his "ladder" of love: one concept or principle that leads from the lowest realm to the highest.

A Platonic ladder is also implied in Book v, but nevertheless the strategy there for transcending the opposition between the cave and the sky is very different. The first four books argue for divine lawfulness in human behavior, and the fifth book argues for human freedom. The texture changes with Book v to one of almost undiluted abstract argument with much less dialogue and poetry. Book v resolves the apparent conflict between God's foreknowledge and human free will through a careful analysis of the nature of know-ing. But this explicit piece of epistemological argu-ment turns out, metaphorically, also to resolve the op-position between the cave and the sky that pervaded Books I–IV.

It is important to follow the steps of the argu-ment. First the common misconception:

"[Y]ou think that if things can be foreseen they must neces-sarily happen." (v, Pr. 4)

Next — the key to the Boethian strategy — the idea that knowledge is a function of the knower as much as of the thing known:

"Now the cause of this error lies in your assumption that whatever is known, is known only by the force and nature of the things which are known; but the opposite is true. Everything which is known is known not according to its own power but rather according to the capacity of the knower." (*Ibid.*)

Four degrees of knowing are distinguished — the senses, imagination, reason, and intelligence:

"The *senses* grasp the figure of the thing as it is constituted in matter; the *imagination,* however, grasps the figure alone without the matter. *Reason,* on the other hand, goes beyond this and investigates by universal consideration the species itself which is in particular things. The vision of *intelligence* is higher yet, and it goes beyond the bounds of the universe and sees with the clear eye of the mind the pure form itself." (*Ibid.;* emphasis added)

Whether or not we like the metaphysics or psychology, we cannot fault the epistemology: that the *human* knowing apparatus cannot know free future events does not mean that some superior knowing apparatus cannot know them. This superior kind of knowing — "the vision of intelligence" — is of course God's kind:

". . . human reason supposes [mistakenly] that the divine intelligence beholds future events only as reason herself sees them. . . . [But] Let us rise, if we can, to the summit of the highest intelligence; for there reason will see what in itself it cannot see: that a certain and definite foreknowledge can behold even those things which have no certain outcome. And this foreknowledge is not mere conjecture but the unrestricted simplicity of supreme knowledge." (v, Pr. 5)

In short, God's foreknowledge is a nonhuman kind of knowledge which does not undermine human free will at all.[20]

In itself this could be called a nonargument. After all, almost nothing is beyond the realm of possibility. The interesting point here — and I think it explains why so many readers have felt that Boethius is making sense and not just pulling a piece of arbitrary magic out of the sky — is the way Boethius *explains* God's "intelligence." Boethius explains the difference between the third and fourth degrees of knowing by distinguishing between time and eternity. Human reason operates from within time, God's knowledge operates outside time from the viewpoint of eternity:

". . . God lives in the eternal present, His knowledge transcends all movement of time and abides in the simplicity of its immediate present. It encompasses the infinite sweep of past and future, and regards all things in its simple comprehension as if they were now taking place." (v, Pr. 6)

This distinction between knowing from time and knowing from eternity depends, in turn, on a visual-spatial model for knowing: knowing as seeing. God's knowing from eternity or outside time — the fourth degree of knowing — is like seeing from a great height. Everything can be seen simultaneously, just as Scipio Africanus could see the whole world with an instantaneous glance from the heavens. On the other hand, knowing from within time — reason, or the third degree of knowing — is like trying to see from no elevation at all and hence being unable to see far "ahead" or "behind." In short, God's kind of knowledge, which does not diminish free will, is explained through the implicit opposition between the cave and the sky — immersion and perspective:

"Let us rise, if we can, to the summit of the highest intelligence; for there reason will see what in itself it cannot see." (v, Pr. 5)

"The vision of intelligence is higher yet, and it goes beyond the bounds of the universe and sees with the clear eye of the mind the pure form itself. . . . With a single glance of the mind it formally, as it were, sees all things." (v, Pr. 4)

". . . divine knowledge . . . resides above all inferior things and looks out on all things from their summit." (v, Pr. 6)

"Just as, when you happen to see simultaneously a man walking on the street and the sun shining in the sky, even though you see both at once, you can distinguish between them and realize that one action is voluntary, the other necessary; so the divine mind, looking down on all things, does not disturb the nature of the things which are present before it but are future with respect to time." (v, Pr. 6)

And so it turns out that what Boethius is talking about in this more conceptual, logical, and rigorous fifth book — careful distinctions between degrees of knowing and between time and eternity — is another way of talking about the metaphorical cave/sky opposition which dominates Books I–IV: the difference between soaring aloft and being pinned down underneath. And here in Book v he shows with self-conscious logic how the sky and the cave are bridged: the four degrees of knowing constitute a ladder linking the sky and the cave. Book v's new rendering and resolution of the cave/sky dichotomy asserts that the immense contradiction between being constrained in the sorrow of the cave and soaring free in the light of the heavens is only the difference between two adjacent modes of knowing (third and fourth). This explains why Book v gives a satisfactory sense of conclusion even though it seems outwardly like a new departure in texture and subject matter.[21]

The model for transcending oppositions that Boethius uses is interestingly hierarchical. The two opposites are not equal or symmetrical: in effect, the cave is contained by or is a subset of the sky. Boethius gives another example to clarify this hierarchical pattern of thinking. He has already explained the distinction between the third and fourth degrees of knowing — human reason from within time and divine intelligence from eternity. Now, to illustrate the difference between the second and third modes — imagination and reason — he resolves the problem of whether universals really exist. Here too he shows that what looks like contradiction is only the subset relationship between two degrees of knowing:

"What, then, should we think if the senses and imagination were to oppose reason by arguing that the universal, which reason claims to know, is nothing? Suppose they were to argue that whatever can be sensed or imagined cannot be universal; and that therefore either the judgment of reason is true, and there are no objects of sense knowledge, or, since everyone knows that many things can be known by the senses and the imagination, that the conception of reason, which regards whatever is sensible and singular as if it were universal, is vain and empty. And suppose, further, that reason should answer that it conceives sensible and imaginable objects under the aspect of universality, but that the senses and imagination cannot aspire to the knowledge of universality because their knowledge cannot go beyond corporeal figures. Moreover, reason might continue, in matters of knowledge we ought to trust the stronger and more perfect judgment. In such a controversy we who possess the power of reason, as well as of imagination and sense perception, ought to take the side of reason." (v, Pr. 5)[22]

In transcending oppositions Boethius does not make the two sides precisely equal. He clearly maintains that God's knowing is higher than human reason, and that reason, in perceiving universals, is higher than sense and imagination, which fail to perceive them. But he shows that the sense of polar opposition is mistaken, and that the seemingly contradictory elements in the opposition can be reconciled through seeing one as a subset of the other (" 'In all this we chiefly observe that the higher power of knowing includes the lower, but the lower can in no way rise to the higher' " [v, Pr. 4]). He also removes the sense of an unbridgeable gulf separating the two elements by showing that they are not just adjacent, but adjacent knowings of the *same* reality. In short, he implies that the normal sense of contradiction in these oppositions comes from the limitations of human language, thought, and perception.

Boethius uses this same hierarchical strategy to reconcile the opposition between Providence and Fate.[23] These two concepts, which most contemporaries saw as irreconcilable, Boethius shows as two knowings of the same reality. One involves a loftier and more inclusive understanding:

"Thus Providence is the unfolding of temporal events as this is present to the vision of the divine mind; but this same unfolding of events as it is worked out in time is called Fate. . . . Therefore, the changing course of Fate is to the simple stability of Providence as reasoning is to intellect, as that which is generated to that which *is,* as time is to eternity, as a circle to its center." (IV, Pr. 6)

In describing Dame Philosophy's robe, Boethius uses a miniature allegorical transcending of the philosophical contradiction between *theory* and *practice*. This passage emphasizes the Platonic ladder that I think is always implicit in these transcendings:

"At the lower edge of her robe was woven a Greek π, at the top the letter θ, and between them were seen clearly marked stages, like stairs, ascending from the lowest level to the highest." (I, Pr. 1)

Another example, because it is not so neatly worked out, indicates how this pattern of thinking seemed to come naturally to Boethius' mind. Here he is bridging, in five stages, the opposition between the freedom of the sky and the freedom of the cave, which feels like slavery:

"But I do not say that this freedom is the same in all beings. [1] In supreme and divine substances there is clear judgment, uncorrupted will, and effective power to obtain what they desire. [2] Human souls, however, are more free while they are engaged in contemplation of the divine mind, and [3] less free when they are joined to bodies, and [4] still less free when they are bound by earthly fetters. [5] They are in utter slavery when they lose possession of their reason and give themselves wholly to vice." (V, Pr. 2; numbers added)

Boethius' bent for transcending oppositions can be said to derive naturally and logically from his views on being and knowing. Or perhaps his philosophical views derive from his habits of thinking. About being his view is that all things are ultimately one:

"What nature has made simple and indivisible, human error has divided. . . . Human depravity, then, has broken into fragments that which is by nature one and simple; men try to grasp part of a thing which has no parts and so get neither the part, which does not exist, nor the whole, which they do not seek." (III, Pr. 9)

Seemingly disparate things, then, relate to each other not so much by logic or meaning, but rather by *partaking* of each other. For example:

"[M]en become happy by *acquiring* divinity. . . . Thus everyone who is happy *is* a god and, although it is true that God is one by nature, still there may be many gods by *participation*." (III, Pr. 10; emphasis added)

About knowledge, his view could be called cognitive relativity: "Everything which is known is known not according to its own power but rather according to the capacity of the knower" (v, Pr. 4). Thus human perception and language are not fitted to grasp things at their deepest (unitary) level:

"The human mind, overcome by the body's blindness, cannot discern by its dim light the delicate connections between things." (v, Met. 3)

" 'But it is hard for me to recount all this as if I were a God,' for it is not fitting for men to understand intellectually or to explain verbally all the dispositions of the divine work." (IV, Pr. 6)

For this reason it is natural that the human search for truth, if it gets very far, should lead to contradiction:

"What cause of discord breaks the ties which ought to bind this union of things? What God has set such conflict between these two truths? Separately each is certain, but put together they cannot be reconciled. Is there no discord between them? Can they exist side by side and be equally true?" (V, Met. 3)

And therefore contradiction is not something to avoid but to pursue:

"But now let us set our arguments against each other and perhaps from their opposition some special truth will emerge." (III, Pr. 12)

By transcending certain oppositions deliberately, and sometimes not deliberately — by characteristically assuming truth on both sides of the contradiction — Boethius gets further than most thinkers did in overcoming the limitations of language, thought, and the single human point of view.

II. *TROILUS AND CRISEYDE*[24]

CHAUCER calls attention to the problem of freedom and necessity in Troilus' long speech in Book IV (958–1082), and to the problem of whether true happiness is possible on earth in Criseyde's briefer speech in Book III (813–40).[25] These speeches may violate what we think of as realism; they may seem like abstract digressions; they are variously disparaged;[26] yet clearly they are deliberate. Chaucer goes out of his way in them to drop his principal source, Boccaccio's narrative, and bring in philosophical material from Boethius (*Consolation of Philosophy,* v, Pr. 2 and 3; II, Pr. 4).[27] These two philosophical speeches are in fact central to the narrative poem as a whole.

I shall argue that the reader who does not settle prematurely upon a final interpretation tends to respond to these speeches in three stages: first agreeing with them, then disagreeing and seeing them ironically, and finally seeing an irony in that very irony and agreeing with the speeches more profoundly than at first. The result of this process, and what is important about it, is that after agreeing, disagreeing, and agreeing again, both positions somehow remain affirmed. Simple irony is saying one thing and meaning another. What haunts in Chaucer is his ability to mean both —

to have it both ways. The final problem is the problem of Chaucerian irony: there is no joke.

The burden of Troilus' speech is that "al that comth, comth by necessitee" (IV, 958). He is also concerned with two corollaries: generally, that all men lack free will (1059), and specifically, that it is his destiny to be forsaken by Criseyde (959).

At first the reader simply accepts as serious argument and rhetoric Troilus' insistence on necessity. After all, the same sentiments are repeated in many different ways throughout the poem, not only by Troilus and sometimes Pandarus, but also by the poet himself. For example, Book IV, which contains the speech, opens by ascribing the whole shape of the narrative to Fortune and her wheel:

> But al to litel, weylaway the whyle,
> Lasteth swich joie, ythonked be Fortune,
> That semeth trewest whan she wol bygyle,
> And kan to fooles so hire song entune,
> That she hem hent and blent, traitour commune!
> And whan a wight is from hire whiel ythrowe,
> Than laugheth she, and maketh hym the mowe.
>
> From Troilus she gan hire brighte face
> Awey to writhe, and tok of hym non heede,
> But caste hym clene out of his lady grace,
> And on hire whiel she sette up Diomede;
> For which right now myn herte gynneth blede,
> And now my penne, allas! with which I write,
> Quaketh for drede of that I moste endite.
>
> (IV, 1–14)

Two stanzas near the beginning of the poem run the gamut of rhetorical clothing for these sentiments:

> O blynde world, O blynde entencioun!
> How often falleth al the effect contraire
> Of surquidrie and foul presumpcioun;
> For kaught is proud, and kaught is debonaire.
> This Troilus is clomben on the staire,
> And litel weneth that he moot descenden;
> But alday faileth thing that fooles wenden.
>
> As proude Bayard gynneth for to skippe
> Out of the weye, so pryketh hym his corn,
> Till he a lasshe have of the longe whippe;
> Than thynketh he, "Though I praunce al byforn
> First in the trays, ful fat and newe shorn,
> Yet am I but an hors, and horses lawe
> I moot endure, and with my feres drawe";
>
> (I, 211–24)

The sense of necessity is increased in yet other ways. Through the lens of courtly love, the poet pictures Troilus first as carefree and scornful of lovers and then as struck down helplessly at his first sight of Criseyde. There was no choice. And Criseyde, at her first sight of Troilus, exclaims, "Who yaf me drynke?" (II, 651). In addition, Chaucer portrays the love story against the deeply fated story of Troy. Professor Curry notes these and many other direct and indirect references to fate, fortune, and destiny, and he concludes with Troilus that "an absolutely inescapable necessity governs the progress of the story."[28]

But the poem leads the reader past this initial

agreement with Troilus. The psychological context, for example, casts the speech in an ironic light. The speech really tells more about Troilus than about freedom and necessity. It does not just say that he is despairing and looking for death; it actually undermines the sense of necessity. For Troilus has already fully despaired, and has been put back on his feet by Pandarus with a plan for staying with Criseyde (IV, 220–658). Yet though there is no subsequent bad news, the speech shows him giving up again. Troilus feels fortune as a powerful, active force pressing him to the ground and himself as powerless to resist. But the reader sees only Troilus' tendency to give up.

If we move from this psychological point of view to a logical view, we continue to question the literal meaning of the speech. It slides quickly into a discussion of whether the necessity of events derives from God's foreknowledge or merely from the fact that events had to happen (IV, 1008–15). But the question of why they had to happen seems to be avoided. It is not a question of what Chaucer *proves* but rather a question of whether he gives the reader a greater *sense* of freedom or necessity. For though Troilus' philosophical language creates a logical frame of reference, the problem of freedom and necessity in the poem cannot be settled on purely logical grounds. *Necessity* and *freedom* are not rigorously enough defined to tell us whether each entirely excludes the other. Perhaps the two overlap.

From an historical point of view we see these arguments for determinism, taken nearly verbatim from Boethius, are quoted without the Boethian context that goes on to refute Troilus and demonstrate free will. Chaucer gives Troilus arguments that Boethius set up for the purpose of knocking down.[29]

In short, the speech makes better dramatic that philosophic sense. Troilus grasps the issue firmly in the first two lines, but then he gnaws and worries at it with fierce, adolescent efforts to reason closely, until the whole matter ends up muddy. Troilus further undermines his speech by praying at the very end for Jove to make it all come out better (IV, 1079–82). (In Boethius, the passage goes on to say it is pointless to hope or pray for anything.)

Narrative technique adds to this ironic reading of the speech. Some events have too many causes. Events that the poet ascribes to fortune are fully explained otherwise. For example, the poet praises fortune for the smoky rain that forced Criseyde to stay overnight at Pandarus' house:

> But O Fortune, executrice of wyrdes!
> O influences of thise hevenes hye!
> Soth is, that under God ye ben oure hierdes,
> Though to us bestes ben the causes wrie.
> This mene I now, for she gan homward hye,
> But execut was al bisyde hire leve
> The goddes wil; for which she moste bleve.

> The bente moone with hire hornes pale,
> Saturne, and Jove, in Cancro joyned were,
> That swych a reyn from heven gan avale,
> That every maner womman that was there

Hadde of that smoky reyn a verray feere;
At which Pandare tho lough, and seyde thenne,
"Now were it tyme a lady to gon henne!"

(III, 617–30)

Chaucer did not have to bring Pandarus' chuckle so close on the heels of this lofty apostrophe. And he need not have written, just earlier, that Pandarus waited for a moonless night, and one in which the clouds were piling up for a storm, before inviting Criseyde to dinner (III, 549 ff.).[30] The poet calls further attention to human causes by Criseyde's protest, when invited, that perhaps she had better not come because of the rain (III, 562). Then, at the end of this dinner invitation, Chaucer raises a doubt the reader might never have thought of: whether Criseyde believes Pandarus' story. By raising this question and coyly declining to answer it, Chaucer leaves the doubt uppermost in the reader's mind:

Nought list myn auctour fully to declare
What that she thoughte whan he seyde so,
That Troilus was out of towne yfare,
As if he seyde therof soth or no;
But that, withowten await, with hym to go,
She graunted hym, sith he hire that bisoughte
And, as his nece, obeyed as hire oughte.

(III, 575–81)

Chaucer pinpoints the moment when Criseyde first began to like Troilus more than anyone else, and again gives too many causes. The natural causes suffice: before she sees Troilus ride by, Pandarus has been elaborately and subtly preparing the ground so that the sight of him makes her think fondly of his prowess, social position, renown, intelligence, physique, nobleness, manhood, and most of all his pain and distress (ii, 660 ff.). But Chaucer adds deterministic causes. First of all, the sight of him sinks from her eyes down into her heart and makes her exclaim, "Who yaf me drynke?" as though a force were suddenly acting upon her. Second, Venus is in her seventh house at the time. And third, "sooth to seyne," Venus was no enemy to Troilus at his birth (ii, 650, 680 ff.).

Logically, all these causes *could* work together. Indeed, in the first stage of responding (in a first reading for most people), such passages give no pause. But once suspicion is aroused, the reader is apt to become wary of the etiological congestion and the offhand tone. When an event is attributed to fortune but not described, human causes spring to mind. There are even hints about how to read them in. For example, the reader is told that fortune decided the time had come for a second blissful meeting. The circumstances, the poet says, were the same as before. Those circumstances were indeed memorable, but they involved not so much the agency of fortune as the intricate and careful planning of Pandarus.

Characterization, as well as narrative technique, contributes to an ironic reading of the speech. Though Troilus is almost always passive, if not positively helpless, Chaucer consistently shows Criseyde working actively to maintain freedom and control. If she is led by Pandarus, she takes great care to be led only where she is prepared to go. After each of the many steps in the extended process of her yielding to Troilus, she stops and thinks about what she is doing in order to make sure she is still in control. When the poet gives reasons why she finally consents to see Troilus at Pandarus' house, it is quietly clear that she would not have come except for the secrecy of his coming and the safety of the place (III, 918–24). We know her veto is real because we see her exercise it when Pandarus stages Troilus' passing beneath her window. Pandarus sees that her pity is aroused; he "felte iren hoot and he bygan to smyte" (II, 1276). Would she now consent actually to speak to Troilus to ease his pain? But she says no, there is nothing Pandarus can do, and the affair remains at a standstill for a long while. Indeed, it is the first time the narrative point of view moves back from its close chronological focus to let an indeterminate amount of time pass by (II, 1338–51).

The scene of Criseyde's greatest turmoil is her long internal debate in Book II whether for love she can give up her "maistrye" (II, 690–812). Her anxiety is portrayed not only by the length of the debate but also by gradual, accelerating changes of mind, until finally she can no longer think coherently and goes off "to pleye." She is attracted to Troilus and to love, but "I am myn owene womman . . . Shal noon housebande seyn to me 'chek mat!'/ . . . Allas! syn I am free/ Shoulde I now love, and put in jupartie/My sikernesse, and thrallen libertee?" (II, 750 ff., 771 ff.).

Her solution to this problem gives perhaps the

strongest sense of her freedom: she gives in to love and Troilus because she finds him so obedient, discreet, and sensitive both to her feelings and to her desires (III, 464–82). In short, she loves because she is able to retain autonomy. Chaucer portrays her surrender more as an event that occurs self-consciously within her own mind than as a process of interaction with Troilus. Indeed, Troilus seems rather left out. This impression is confirmed on the first night of love. She undermines the strikingly aggressive tone he achieves on that occasion when she asserts, however sweetly, that she is not letting anything happen to her that she has not already decided on herself:

> [He] "Now be ye kaught, now is there but we twene!
> Now yeldeth yow, for other bote is non!"
> .   .   .   .   .   .
> [She] "Ne hadde I er now, my swete herte deere,
> Ben yold, ywis, I were now nought heere!"
>
> (III, 1207–11)

Her control is later illustrated in their disagreement about whether she should leave Troy: *she* decides.

For all these reasons, the reader is led to an ironic view of Troilus' fatalistic speech. But as the meanings in the speech and the poem develop and interact, I think it is inevitable that the reader will also begin to develop counterresponses. A new irony develops, a deeper sense in which Troilus is *right* to say that all is necessary and men lack free will. This is the third stage of response. There are two sources: our final sense of

Criseyde's character and Chaucer's narrative technique.

Although Criseyde works to maintain control, she is nevertheless ultimately unfree. Her acquiescence to Diomede follows ominously along the same steps as her previous one to Troilus.[31] There is the same slow capitulation involving many small steps over a long period of time; she characteristically asserts her control by refusing the favor asked while granting a smaller one of her own choosing; and when she tells Diomede that he may visit but may not speak of love (v, 950), we can piece together the whole process, for it was by just such degrees that Troilus won her. She is perfectly sincere in such actions; she is not playing coy games. The matter lies deeper. Her own insistence on agency and control actually serves to hide from herself the fact that she will always give in to sufficient importunity and shrewdness — the qualities of Troilus and Pandarus that Diomede so happily combines. Though she always finds a moment to check with herself that the man is admirable and worthy (v, 1023–29; ii, 659–65), her response is "pite" (v, 824), one of the highest courtly virtues. Always she "means well" (*e. g.,* v, 1004). Thus her bemusement at the end is genuine: she does not know how it all happened; she does not feel it is her doing.

This deeper absence of freedom in Criseyde is clarified by describing two different ways in which she could have avoided treachery. At first glance it seems that *too much* freedom led her to unfaithfulness: if she had surrendered more of it to Troilus and followed his advice, they would have lived happily ever after. But it is just as accurate to blame her *lack of freedom:* in order to remain faithful while among the Greeks, she would have had to make a strong positive act, and this is precisely what she somehow lacks the freedom or agency to do. Though in control at any moment, she is powerless in the long run. Is this only a manipulation of the truism that people act as they do because of their characters? If so, the manipulation is Chaucer's, and he saves it from emptiness. For by his portrayal of her character and by his shaping of the narrative, he creates an ultimate sense of necessity in the way Criseyde responds to Troilus and Diomede — a sense of determinism even in her guarding her freedom at every individual moment.

So too Chaucer's distancing narrative technique in this latter part of the poem gives a sense of necessity. In the first three books the progress of the affair is atomized into tiny, chronological steps, with full focus on the present and none on the past or future, but in Books IV and V Chaucer imposes a detached view that gives a sense of destiny. In the first three books not even the narrator seems to know what will happen next, but here the reader is constantly forced to watch the slow coming to pass of what he already knows and rues.

The most striking instance is the loud opening of Book IV, where the poet announces that fortune began to set up Diomede on her wheel. The narrative structure of Book V intensifies the same effect. Chaucer starts by watching Criseyde ride out of Troy with

Diomede, follows her, and shows at the end of her
journey that though she is sad and thinks only of
Troilus, she nonetheless consents to give a familiarly
civil response to Diomede's subtle urging (v, 1–196).
Even in this he quietly suggests the end and the process leading to it. Next, staying in chronological order,
he moves the reader back to Troy to watch Troilus for
the first nine days of his wait (v, 197–686). But toward
the end of that period he gives another suggestion of
how things will work out: at Troilus' eager anticipa-
tion of her return, Pandarus mutters, "Ye, hase wode!
. . ./God woot, refreyden may this hote fare,/Er Calkas
sende Troilus Criseyde!" (v, 505–8). Then, again not
breaking the time sequence, the reader is moved back
to Criseyde to watch her thinking on the ninth day
that she will return to Troilus no matter what the
consequences (v, 687–770). But in the middle of this
thought, in the middle of a scene, and in the middle
of a stanza — and after three scene changes that have
not broken the smooth flow of time — the narrator in-
trudes to jolt the reader ahead to the end of the whole
story. Criseyde forgets Troy and Troilus:

> "But natheles, bityde what bityde,
> I shal to-morwe at nyght, by est or west,
> Out of this oost stele, on some manere syde,
> And gon with Troilus where as hym lest.
> This purpos wol ich holde, and this is best.
> No fors of wikked tonges janglerie,
> For evere on love han wrecches had envye.
>
> "For whoso wol of every word take hede
> Or reulen hym by every wightes wit,
> Ne shal he nevere thryven, out of drede;

For that that some men blamen evere yit,
Lo, other manere folk comenden it.
And as for me, for al swich variaunce,
Felicite clepe I my suffisaunce.

"For which, withouten any wordes mo,
To Troie I wole, as for conclusioun."
But God it wot, er fully monthes two,
She was ful fer fro that entencioun!
For bothe Troilus and Troie town
Shal knotteles thoroughout hire herte slide;
For she wol take a purpos for t'abyde.

(v, 750–70)

By nesting one story inside another, Chaucer makes this explicit revelation serve as the ending not just of one story but of two. For now the focus moves back, not to the Criseyde-Troilus story that was in progress, but to the interleaved Criseyde-Diomede story. Only after watching the Criseyde-Diomede story proceed to its already revealed conclusion (v, 771–1099) is the reader carried back a second time to the ninth day, the point at which the modulation occurred. And having already viewed that sad interval of time from the point of view of Jove, the reader must now do so again, watching Troilus' pathetic hope linger on through the long tenth day into the weeks that follow (v, 1100–end). The vantage point imposed by this narrative technique contributes to the final sense of necessity already suggested by the handling of Criseyde's character — contributes, that is, to final agreement with Troilus' fatalistic speech.[32]

The three stages of responding may sound too neat. But they represent the three levels of complexity

that actually inhere in the meanings of the words of
the poem. The second step, seeing the fatalistic speech
ironically, builds on the initial agreement with the
literal message of the speech; the third step, more profound agreement with its determinism, is more profound precisely because it takes account of and builds
on the ironic second response. My premise here is that
we cannot give an account of the meaning of complex
language without bringing in the time dimension.

Criseyde's philosophical speech is parallel in many
ways to Troilus'. His denies the possibility of human
freedom, hers of human happiness. Both are from
Boethius, but both are what Dame Philosophy shows
to be cries of erroneous despair. And both speeches
elicit the same three stages of reponse. In fact, the
two come to function together at the end of the poem.

"There is no verray weele in this world heere"
(III, 836). At first we naturally assent because her
speech is effective and seems to fit the poem. It is
shorter, firmer, and clearer than Troilus'. No obvious
irony. It closes with the same logical device Troilus
uses: asserting that all possibilities can be gathered
into an either/or set, and then showing that the same
conclusion follows from both:

> "Either he woot that thow, joie, art muable,
> Or woot it nought; it mot been oon of tweye.
> Now if he woot it nought, how may he seye
> That he hath verray joie and selynesse,
> That is of ignoraunce ay in derknesse?

"Now if he woot that joie is transitorie,
As every joie of wordly thyng mot flee,
Than every tyme he that hath in memorie,
The drede of lesing maketh hym that he
May in no perfit selynesse be."

(III, 822–31)

The neat alternatives are further believable because they fit Troilus so well. He *is* so ignorant of how transitory his happiness is, both in the beginning when he scorns love, and at the height of his happiness with Criseyde. And when he is hoping and expecting that she will return from the Greeks, his ignorance is even more touching. Yet — turning to the other logical possibility — during that period when they are together but he knows she must leave, and knows thus that their joy must be transitory, this knowledge *does* destroy for him any possibility of happiness in their remaining time.

Thus, like Troilus' speech, Criseyde's is first accepted on its own terms as serious rhetoric carrying simple, abstract truth value for the poem. But as with Troilus' speech, the reader will begin to sense an ironic reading when he begins to sense its paradoxical relation to its context in the poem. These somber, lofty philosophical reflections are undermined by the circumstances which prompt them: Pandarus' most gratuitously trumped-up story of jealousy in his elaborate staging to bring the lovers happily to bed. Criseyde's bleak pessimism is further undermined by a grave joy that permeates Book III. The speech stands near the center of the book, which Chaucer distinguished from the others by an elegant symmetry among passages of joy. Lofty hymns to love and harmony open and close the book, and the consummation of their love is intensely rendered at the center.[38] In portraying this extended scene, Chaucer emphasizes the *perfection* of the very joy that her speech tries to deny the possibility of. He even addresses consciously the question of how to express perfect joy:

> Nought nedeth it to yow, syn they ben met,
> To axe at me if that they blithe were;
> For if it erst was wel, tho was it bet
> A thousand fold; this nedeth nought enquere.
> Agon was every sorwe and every feere;
> And bothe ywis, they hadde, and so they wende,
> As muche joie as herte may comprende.
>
> This is no litel thyng of for to seye;
> This passeth every wit for to devyse;
> For ech of hem gan otheres lust obeye.
> Felicite, which that thise clerkes wise
> Comenden so, ne may nought here suffise;
> This joie may nought writen be with inke;
> This passeth al that herte may bythynke.
>
> (III, 1681–94)

The ironic view of her speech is confirmed if the reader notices its relation to context in Boethius: like Troilus' speech, it offers the very view that Boethius is striving to deny — in this case, a wrong conception of happiness (see *Consolation*, II, Pr. 4).

But even though this affirmation of transcendent earthly joy at the center of the poem is very powerful and penetrating, all the elements of the poem make us move beyond this ironic perception of her speech. As the meanings continue to adjust and readjust themselves, we come around again to agree with Criseyde that earthly happiness is impossible.

One of the main elements that produces this third response is the wry comedy throughout, and especially the fairly broad comedy in Book III.[34] Their happy love is given there in a comic perspective that distances the reader. Chaucer proceeds to the passionate consummation by a path strewn with ridiculous and trivial details of physical indignity and psychological frailty. By adding a comic point of view, Chaucer increases the size and complexity of the world, and in doing so he diminishes the relative scale of the consummation: at Criseyde's loving reproach Troilus faints; while he is unconscious, she and Pandarus undress him and put him to bed with her; and as they rub his wrists, he is shocked and frightened to wake up naked in bed with a woman — circumstances traditionally called blissful. In addition to this near slapstick, there is a constant sense of Pandarus' presence to heighten the reader's sense of self as spectator. Significantly, these distancing elements — physical comedy, ironic lines, and the sense of Pandarus' presence — are not in Boccaccio's story, which Chaucer has been following closely.

Those distancing elements are probably not enough to make most readers agree again with Criseyde's denial of the possibility of happiness. Her speech is only fully reaffirmed with the ending of the poem. But this ending functions in a complex way. Though it reaffirms her speech, what is more significant here is that it both *denies and affirms* — and not only her speech but Troilus' too. To show this I shall go back a step in the dialectical process to demonstrate how the ending denies the speeches, and then I shall discuss its affirming effect.

The ending of the poem is Boethian: it denies the speeches, or corrects them, just as Dame Philosophy did in the *Consolation.* At the end of the poem, Troilus has Dame Philosophy's elevated vantage point, and he clearly tells the reader that there *is* freedom or free will, that men bear responsibility for their actions, and that they are free to seek the true good and shun the false. The poet explicitly joins in:

> O yonge, fresshe folkes, he or she,
> In which that love up groweth with youre age,
> Repeyreth hom fro worldly vanyte,
> And of youre herte up casteth the visage
> To thilke God that after his ymage
> Yow made.

> (v, 1835-40)

Nor is this just abstract "doctrine." The fact that most readers retain a sense of Criseyde's guilt shows that a sense of free will has actually been transmitted. (Chaucer does not fully excuse her: he hedges, *e. g.,* in v, 1093-99, 1772-85.)

The ending of the poem denies or corrects Criseyde's speech too: people *can* be truly happy if they set their hearts on the true good and stop hankering after the false:

And in hymself he lough right at the wo
Of hem that wepten for his deth so faste;
And dampned al oure werk that foloweth so
The blynde lust, the which that may nat laste
And sholden al oure herte on heven caste.

(v, 1821–25)

For he [Christ] nyl falsen no wight, dar I seye,
That wol his herte al holly on hym leye.

(v, 1845–46)

This ending is built on Boethian images of free-dom: to "repeyren" home (late Latin *repatriare*), to look down on the earth from a great distance, and to see clearly. Chaucer uses explicitly here the episode from Cicero/Macrobius that Boethius evokes. The ending functions like Book v of the *Consolation* in that it also implies (imaginatively instead of with Boethius' logic) that it is wrong to associate necessity with foreknowledge. *True* vision, true *perspective* — i. e., Troilus' view from the eighth sphere — reveals freedom, not necessity. The earlier images of perspective or detachment may have seemed to suggest necessity, but they were incomplete. Pandarus embodies this incomplete perspective, this detachment which misleads: his vicarious way of living and his spectator's point of view produce, finally, a mood of resignation and a sense of the impossibility of true happiness. Thus the ending is a Boethian corrective to Troilus' denial of freedom and Criseyde's denial of happiness.

But on the other hand, this Boethian ending, in the complex way Chaucer uses it, serves at the same time to *affirm* the speeches of Troilus and Criseyde.

That is to say, even though this soaring out to the point of view of the eighth sphere gives a taste of true detachment, a taste of true freedom and true happiness, Chaucer is less austere and more romantic than Boethius. He does not carry *us* fully to the eighth sphere and the heavenly point of view, as Boethius carries us fully into Dame Philosophy's point of view at the end of the *Consolation*. Throughout the poem we think we are able to take a comfortably detached view of these affairs. So often we share Pandarus' perspective and look down with an understanding smile upon these doings, as we laugh with him at the efforts of the lovers to bring themselves to bliss. But the ending turns the tables, and Troilus has the laugh on us. His distance and perspective in looking down on us surpass ours in looking down on his dismay when he found himself in bed with Criseyde. When Chaucer finally shows *true* detachment or perspective, he does not make it fully *our* view. It is beyond mortality. Of course we understand, accept, and perhaps even vicariously enjoy Troilus' heavenly point of view. But essentially we are left weeping below. Chaucer makes us feel the inevitable constraint and necessity in our earthy station:

> "Yet am I but an hors, and horses lawe
> I moot endure, and with my feres drawe";
>
> (I, 223–24)

The ending similarly reaffirms Criseyde's speech. Though it leaves us truly believing that we should reject "brotel" goods, the poem has given us such an overwhelming experience of immersion in the earthly point of view that we cannot so easily give it up. Being told so suddenly to reject those things we have been so deeply immersed in — though it causes only a few readers actually to *reject* the heavenly view as an excrescence on the poem — certainly does make us feel how much we do not yet *share* this heavenly view. Part of the power of those litanylike stanzas of renunciation and condemnation derives from their also serving a fond mourning and sorrowing function:[35]

> Swich fyn hath, lo, this Troilus for love!
> Swich fyn hath al his grete worthynesse!
> Swich fyn hath his estat real above,
> Swich fyn his lust, swich fyn hath his noblesse!
> Swich fyn hath false worldes brotelnesse!
>
> .   .   .   .   .   .
>
> Lo here, of payens corsed olde rites,
> Lo here, what alle hire goddes may availle;
> Lo here, thise wrecched worldes appetites;
> Lo here, the fyn and guerdoun for travaille
> Of Jove, Appollo, of Mars, of swich rascaille!
> Lo here, the forme of olde clerkis speche
> In poetrie, if ye hire bokes seche.
>
> (v, 1828–32, 1849–55)

The reason why this ending is so disputed is that it affirms true freedom and true happiness in a way that also confirms our feelings of constraint and sadness.[36]

The simplest way to describe Chaucer's irony is to say that he renders events from two vantage points instead of just one and that the two renderings seem to supplement each other. Chaucer shows how love looks from a distance without denying how it feels from up close. He reinforces this effect through the points of view of Pandarus and the narrator. The reader does not simply see events through the naive and pious eyes of the narrator — a view from up close. The ironic point of view of Pandarus is too strong. Yet the reader cannot help but feel the limitation of Pandarus' detachment. The presence and the technique of the narrator lend a naiveté and innocence which Pandarus lacks, so that the reader is better able to become involved and to participate in the love and joy.

By using these somewhat phenomenological terms — by talking about how love looks from near and far — we understand Chaucer's achievement as a rendering of the complexity of life: events are both *experienced* (from within) and *perceived* (from without). We think of Chaucer's poetry more as language that conforms to the way things are (good mimesis) than as language that violates the way we conceptualize things (bad logic). But Chaucer is too interested in philosophical issues to rest content with good mimesis. He conceives his matter not only in narrative and lyric terms but also in philosophical terms, *i. e.,* as instances of the "problem of freedom" and the "problem of happiness." He could have just told his story, following Boccaccio, and kept the philosophical problems from getting in the way. But he wanted to raise these problems and so he took the trouble to bring in the speeches from Boethius. Many other uses of language in the poem underline this philosophic context and encourage the reader to wonder whether or not people can be free and happy. It turns out, therefore, that Chaucer must violate the laws of discursive language and logic while he is achieving the rich accuracy of mimesis. He must manage both to affirm and to deny that people can be truly free and happy.

It is by means of poetry that generates the three stages of response explored here — agreeing with the speeches, disagreeing, and then agreeing again — that Chaucer preserves the opposite assertions from being undermined by each other. Something will only stay said if it is said in the full light of its opposite. This is the method of simple irony, which uses a contrary statement to express its meaning. Ironic statements are thus difficult to deny or ridicule. Accordingly, in order to affirm not only that all is necessary and sad, but also that there is freedom and happiness, Chaucer makes both assertions ironically. He affirms each through the denial of its contrary. But for this really to work, the contrary must in each case be there first. That is why there are three stages and not two. A denial of the speeches comes only after their truth is sensed. And final agreement comes only after their ironic value is truly and irrevocably seen.

Good readers of Chaucer warn against reading him as more openly funny or cute than he is. Though we intuitively recognize the distortion when someone else makes it, it is an easy one to fall into. Now it is clear why. The building block of Chaucer's dialectic here is simple irony: serious statement that the context ridicules. But by compounding this simple irony with another upon it, Chaucer radically deepens the response to the whole. Out of ironic steps, at times even puckish ones, he builds a final serious response. This explains why the characteristic effect of Chaucer's best poetry is not broadly funny, even though comedy plays such a large role, and why he is not negative in his irony, nor finally sentimental in his affirmativeness. For by creating the three responses, Chaucer affirms both positions and denies nothing. Yet he is unsentimental, clear-sighted, and precise because he only affirms ironically.

In *The Knight's Tale* the opposition is an actual contest between two men. Early in the tale Chaucer establishes an evenly balanced *demande d'amour* between Palamon and Arcite: which of them loves Emelye more? which deserves her more? which suffers more? In short, which is the worthier? This traditional chivalric form, the "love problem," serves as the structural framework for the poem. Chaucer formulates the problem in Part I in the simplest and most abstract way by focusing upon these two men in their prison tower and emphasizing their similarity through structurally balanced details. The initial statement of the question of love comes at the close of Part I and reinforces the symmetrical conundrumlike quality of the conflict:

> Yow loveres axe I now this questioun:
> Who hath the worse, Arcite or Palamoun?
> That oon may seen his lady day by day,
> But in prison he moot dwelle alway;
> That oother wher hym list may ride or go,
> But seen his lady shal he nevere mo.
>
> (I, 1347–52)

The question is made more complex in Part II, partly through narrative complication in which Palamon's escape is balanced against Arcite's return in disguise, and partly through the added presence of Emelye and Theseus, whose perceptions and involvement complicate the reader's response to the question.

In Part III the scope of the dilemma is vastly enlarged along physical, social, and theological lines. Physically it is no longer a fight between two men in a virgin grove but a tournament of two hundred knights in a large and elaborate architectural structure before an audience of thousands. All society now takes part. The competitors constitute a polarization of fighting men the world over; the best workers, craftsmen, and artists of the kingdom have made the arena; and the tournament is a major public ritual involving the interest and sympathy of even the commoners. The expansion is even greater in the theological dimension: what was originally a dispute between two men is now a dispute between the planets and their influences.

This expansion of the rather small and neat *demande d'amour* gives a sense that a wide range of forces in society and the universe all converge upon two small men — down upon a "litel spot of erthe." Chaucer adds to this focused shape of things by placing both the tournament and the funeral in the same virgin grove where Palamon and Arcite first fought.

By the end of Part III the question of love between Palamon and Arcite has pulled most of the poem's elements into balanced opposition. This is most striking in the loud contrasts between Venus and Mars, between their temples, and between Emetreus and

Lygurge. Chaucer gives these two leading knights the physical characteristics that Boccaccio, in the source, had given the two lovers.

These symmetries are obvious enough. But about the differences between Palamon and Arcite there is considerable dispute among commentators. Though the differences are subtle, they are important. Palamon is a bit more open, impulsive, and naive than his cousin. This is seen in the impulsive tone of his initial declaration of love for Emelye, his naive uncertainty about whether she is mortal, his ingenuous surprise when Arcite decides to love her as well, and his blurted response when Theseus discovers them fighting in the grove:

> "Sire, what nedeth wordes mo?
> We have the deeth disserved bothe two.
> Two woful wrecches been we, two caytyves,
> That been emcombred of oure owene lyves;"
>
> (I, 1715–18)

He is breathlessly pious. His prayer in Part III is more open and supplicating than Arcite's. For example:

> I am so confus that I kan noghte seye
> But, "Mercy, lady bright, that knowest weele
> My thought, and seest what harmes that I feele!"
>
> (I, 2230–32)

Arcite is discernibly more tough-minded and less open. He would never mistake Emelye for a goddess; he does not just argue for an exception to his oath of brotherhood with Palamon (I, 1152 ff.), he actually defies it (I, 1604 ff.). "Who shal yeve a lovere any lawe," he says (I, 1164), and what he means is something rather curtly pragmatic.

> "And therfor, at the kynges court, my brother,
> Ech man for hymself, ther is noon oother.
> Love, if thee list, for I love and ay shal;"
>
> (I, 1181–83)

His speeches contain confident explanations (*e. g.*, I, 1086 ff., 1153, 1158 ff., 1162 ff.), but Palamon deals typically in bewildered questions and complaints. Palamon, baffled, prays in effect, not for victory, or reputation, or even life itself, but just for Emelye. Arcite, on the other hand, prays directly for victory and does so with composure.

Arcite uses more proverbs than Palamon does. This suggests Arcite's gift for seeing events in perspective or with detachment, while Palamon always seems immersed and without perspective, almost overwhelmed by what is going on. A proverb comes from perspective — it is a standing back and seeing the present event as an instance of a traditional category.

> "And therfor, at the kynges court, my brother,
> Ech man for hymself, ther is noon oother."
>
> (I, 1181–82)

Arcite's language even has a tendency to put things into *reductive* perspective:

We stryve as dide the houndes for the boon;
They foughte al day, and yet hir part was noon.
Ther cam a kyte, whil that they were so wrothe,
And baar awey the boon betwixe hem bothe."

(I, 1177–80)

"We faren as he that dronke is as a mous.
A dronke man woot wel he hath an hous,
But he noot which the righte wey is thider,
And to a dronke man the wey is slider.
And certes, in this world so faren we;"

(I, 1261–65)

This ability to attain a bit more perspective explains why Arcite has a more stoic view of necessity (I, 1086 ff.), and Palamon, by contrast, complains uncomprehendingly about necessity (1303 ff.).[38] On one occasion, Arcite does complain of his fortune (1251 ff.), but as soon as he voices his complaint, he transforms it into a speech which aphoristically *criticizes* people who complain of their fortunes.

But there is a lesson in the fact that Chaucer takes away from Palamon and Arcite the physical differences that Boccaccio had given them. For Chaucer, what is central is their similarity. All the symmetries that Chaucer gives to Boccaccio's diffuse narrative enforce the similarity of the two lovers. Thus, even if open and breathless humility seems attractive, it is going too far to conclude that Palamon is a worthier knight than his cousin or more deserving of Emelye. One could just as well argue that Arcite's clearer thinking and tough-mindedness make him the worthier.[39]

Clearly the two love her equally. They are equally
loyal. There is no reason to doubt Theseus' statement
that they show equal valor, for Chaucer succeeds in
describing the long battle and Arcite's victory without
at all disparaging Palamon's strength, valor, or skill —
or even the qualities of Palamon's knights. Chaucer
balances almost every description or speech of Palamon with a comparable one of Arcite. By pitting
against each other two knights so equally matched,
Chaucer creates a kind of Rorschach test that force-
fully elicits often very intense subjective partisan responses. But even the sharpness of these responses, I
think, comes from the awareness that the two knights
are in fact equally worthy.

The plain truth is that the question asked in Part i
and deepened in Parts ii and iii — which is the worthier? — gets no answer. The following paradoxes constitute Chaucer's refusal to answer: (1) Arcite wins
Emelye, yet Palamon gets her. (2) The final note is on
a wedding, yet its mood is overshadowed by the funeral that precedes it. (3) Arcite wins her by conduct
more fitting to Palamon — fair and square, according
to the rules — even though he was "at the king's court"
and even though he proclaimed himself, as a lover,
above "positif" law. Yet Palamon finally gets her
through an event that has more of Arcite's pragmatic
flavor to it — the intervention of the monster.

How does Chaucer manage to satisfy the reader
while failing to answer the *demande d'amour* on

which the whole poem is built? How does he create a satisfactory sense of conclusion by the end of Part IV? The answer is that the poem builds — especially in Part IV — a bigger and richer world, one in which the conventionally posed love problem seems insufficient or unsatisfactory as a way of understanding life. The tactic, in short, is to face the reader with a problem — the *demande d'amour* — and then to show, dialectically, that the problem is the problem.[40] The way Chaucer enlarges the world and deepens the level of discourse is through Theseus, Saturn, and the final First-Mover speech. I shall explore each in turn.

Theseus is the richest character in the poem. He is mature and experienced, and in this respect he is like the knight who tells this tale. Both are idealized but rendered with strokes of concrete specificity: Theseus, through the homely conversational language he uses; the knight, through the list of real battles he fought in and the fact that his "gypoun" is still "bismotered" from these campaigns. The contrast between Theseus and the two young cousins is like that between the knight and his squire. The older men are seen as having been through it all. Where Arcite succeeds in the realm of war, and Palamon — ultimately — in the realm of love, Theseus is introduced at the start as having succeeded in both.

Theseus enriches the world of the poem especially by the amount of order and ceremony he brings to the bare *demand d'amour* that he uncovers by accident. He is angry that the two men fight alone without judges or rules. The reader is made to feel that the

elaborate tournament grows both physically and cere-
monially out of his will. The ceremoniousness of the
funeral grows similarly from his decrees.

Is it only that Theseus brings the principle of
order? It cannot be that simple. He changes his mind
too often. Rather, he insists on giving a public dimension to private actions: he involves the whole kingdom, even the whole world, and brings a transcendent
dimension to the events in Part III. He twice says that
he wants the tournament so that destiny or fortune can
better work itself out with respect to Palamon and
Arcite (I, 1841–43, 1857–61). Indeed, Chaucer associates Theseus with destiny itself (I, 1661–78).[41] Thus
Theseus serves to give complex embodiment to a conflict otherwise narrowly and abstractly defined — he
"works it out" or "realizes" it. He even makes the
flesh a crucial element by "incarnating" a *demande
d'amour* that had in fact tended to ignore the flesh.
(See below.)

Theseus deepens the level of discourse by bringing into the open and questioning elements implicit
in the *demande d'amour* itself. When he stops the two
lovers from fighting in the grove, he makes us laugh
at what we had assumed admirable till then — that two
knights were ready to fight to the death over a girl
who knew nothing of their love:

> Now looketh, is nat that an heigh folye?
> Who may been a fool, but if he love?
> Bihoold, for Goddes sake that sit above,
> Se how they blede! be they noght wel arrayed?

> Thus hath hir lord, the god of love, ypayed
> Hir wages and hir fees for hir servyse!
> And yet they wenen for to been ful wyse
> That serven love, for aught that may bifalle."
>
> (I, 1798–1805)

He goes on to call love just a game or joke, though till then the poem had encouraged us to respond to it with the utmost seriousness:

> "But this is yet the beste game of alle,
> That she for whom they han this jolitee
> Kan hem therfore as muche thank as me.
> She woot namoore of al this hoote fare,
> By God, than woot a cokkow or an hare!"
>
> (I, 1806–10)

When he changes the rules of the tournament at the last minute in order to avoid killing, he makes us question what we would not have questioned, the very thing implied as glorious — that two hundred knights were ready to kill one another to settle the dispute of Palamon and Arcite. In short, Palamon and Arcite are competing to surpass each other while Theseus — by laughing at their fighting, anger, and love, and by deciding against a mortal tournament — undermines the very criteria for judging their competition, the very criteria that permit us to say which is the worthier.

Theseus increases the reader's sensitivity to bodily injury and decay. Bodily harm almost seems to become a subsidiary theme of the poem. Arcite's disease

and death are described with an instrusive bloodiness.
And when Chaucer ostensibly emphasizes the *preven-
tion* of needless injury, he ends with a gratuitous detail that leaves the sense of pain and perhaps mortal
suffering uppermost in our consciousness:

> And of another thyng they weren as fayn,
> That of hem alle was ther noon yslayn,
> Al were they soore yhurt, and namely oon,
> That with a spere was thirled his brest boon.
>
> (I, 2707–10)

These backhanded emphases upon bodily injury give
a powerful sensory and emotional content to the passage in Theseus' final speech about all things decay-
ing and passing away. The meaning is not merely that
all men die, but that dying is a messy and bloody busi-
ness, and hurts. When there is more felt reality to injury, pain, and death than there is to love — which I
think is true by the end of *The Knight's Tale* — a
demande d'amour begins to lose its footing.

Furthermore, Theseus serves to call into question
the quality of *constancy* implicitly celebrated in the
undying devotion of Palamon and Arcite. Theseus'
most frequent activity is changing his mind. His statements of intention seem sufficiently firm. For example,
speaking of his decision to have the mortal tournament:

> "My wyl is this, for plat conclusioun,
> Withouten any repplicacioun, —
> If that you liketh, take it for the beste:
>
> .   .   .   .   .   .

And this bihote I yow withouten faille,
Upon my trouthe, and as Y am a knyght,

    .   .   .   . .   .

Ye shul noon oother ende with me maken,
That oon of yow ne shal be deed or taken.

And if yow thynketh this is weel ysayd,
Seyeth youre avys, and holdeth you apayd.
This is youre ende and youre conclusioun."

(I, 1845–69)

Yet he changes his mind: about helping the women from Thebes, about releasing Arcite, about killing Palamon and Arcite in the grove, about the rules for the tournament. And his conclusion that Palamon should marry Emelye is like a change of mind: it is a new idea that reverses what he had assumed.

Chaucer builds into Theseus' mind-changing the connotations of sensitive, thoughtful flexibility. This is most noticeable in the passage where Theseus encounters the cousins fighting in the grove (I, 1742–1825). The first lines (I, 1742–61) are like the description of his response to the Theban women who met him at the start of the poem: he was fierce and remorseless until the women pleaded with him to show mercy, and consequently pity ran in his noble heart. But the rest of this long passage reveals how complex this seemingly simple change of mind is.

First, eight lines summarize his mental activity from the outside or with perspective:

And though he first *for ire* quook and sterte,
He hath considered shortly, in a clause,
The trespas of hem bothe, and eek the cause,

And although that *his ire* hir gilt accused,
Yet *in his resoun* he hem bothe excused,
As thus: he *thoghte* wel that every man
Wol helpe hymself in love, if that he kan,
And eek delivere hymself out of prisoun.
(I, 1762–69; emphasis added)

The assertion that it was "in his resoun" that he came to a more merciful conclusion is given weight by the reiteration that it was "his ire" that made him stern.

But next there seems to be an important element of sentiment added to his thought — of "herte" added to "resoun":

And eek *his herte* hadde compassioun
Of wommen, for they wepen evere in oon;
And *in his gentil herte* he thoughte anon,
And softe unto hymself he seyde . . .
(I, 1770–73; emphasis added)

Yet the operation of the "herte" turns out to be strikingly like thinking: weighing, making discriminations and inferences.[42] For Chaucer gives us Theseus' private words to illustrate his heart's activity, and these words emphasize the rational process:

And in his gentil herte he *thoughte* anon,
And softe unto hymself he seyde, "Fy
Upon a lord that wol have no mercy,
But been a leon, bothe in word and dede,
To hem that been in repentaunce and drede,

> As wel as to a proud despitous man
> That wol mayntene that he first bigan.
> That lord hath litel of *discrecioun*,
> That in swich cas kan no *divisioun*,
> But weyeth pride and humblesse after oon."
>
> (I, 1772–81; emphasis added)

Once the emotion of anger is dissipated by the thoughtful process we have just looked at —

> . . . whan his ire is thus agoon,
> He gan to looken up with eyen lighte,
> And spak thise same wordes al on highte:
>
> (I, 1782–84)

— then the way is free for a very different emotion. For the words that he next speaks — out loud now — reveal a new element: humor (I, 1782–1810). The humor involves some detachment. Now that he is over his anger, he can see the situation in perspective and can see its ludicrousness. I have already quoted many of these lines in which he laughs at how "well arrayed" they are in blood, what "jolitee" love inspires, and how Emelye knew nothing of their love and pain.

Next comes a transition to a slightly different texture of humor — warmer and less detached. His humor started out as "laughing at" but it ends up as "laughing with." The change begins with the third line of the following passage:

> "She woot namoore of al this hoote fare,
> By God, than woot a cokkow or an hare!

But all moot ben assayed, hoot and coold;
A man moot ben a fool, or yong or oold, —
I woot it by myself ful yore agon,
For in my tyme a servant was I oon."

(I, 1809–14)

And this warmer humor is, of course, the path to full sympathy (feeling with) and thus finally to genuine, felt forgiveness:

"And therfore, syn I knowe of loves peyne,
And woot hou soore it kan a man distreyne,
As he that hath ben caught ofte in his laas,
I yow foryeve al hoolly this trespas,
At requeste of the queene, that kneleth heere,
And eek of Emelye, my suster deere.
And ye shul bothe anon unto me swere
That nevere mo ye shal my contree dere,
Ne make werre upon me nyght ne day,
But been my freendes in all that ye may.
I yow foryeve this trepas every deel."

(I, 1815–25)

In summary, what looks like a simple change of mind or heart, and is sometimes baldly described as only that, is shown to be a rich sequence of mental processes: from fierce anger, to thoughtful weighing of distinctions (through seeing other people show pity instead of wrath), to intellectual understanding of why the "guilty parties" might have acted as they did, to a comic point of view that reveals the absurdity of their plight, to a warmer humor that identifies with their plight, to feeling with them, and then finally to complete forgiveness.

Needless to say, the reader responds warmly and positively to Theseus in his ability to have such a full and understanding response. Indeed, Theseus displays what seems to be the gift of understanding in the richest sense of the word. The effect of the repeated changes of mind by Theseus — always from fierceness to mercy — is not a simple repudiation of constancy, but rather an endorsement of thoughtfulness, rationality, and the ability thereby to be flexible. Here again Theseus undermines the values implicit in the *demande d'amour:* the poem seems to celebrate the vigor with which the two lovers always respond with the appropriate conventional emotion — immediate love, unbending loyalty, instantly kindled anger, or unswerving fierceness. Yet Theseus implicitly calls into question the value of this simple sort of response. Putting it more positively, Theseus wins greater admiration from us for showing a more complicated, slowly developing reaction, for being able to change his mind and for displaying both the gift for detachment associated with Arcite and the gift for involvement associated with Palamon.

Theseus' final speech also shows him to be richer than the two cousins. The range of emotions in the speech is not large. It moves merely from solemn sadness to solemn acceptance to solemn joy. Yet here again Theseus changes his mind and his actions — un-

doing his vow and persuading Palamon and Emelye
to do likewise — on the strength of a felt, but rational,
mental process. The pivotal line of the speech emphasizes Palamon's conscious use of reason: "What may
I conclude of this longe serye?" (I, 3067). Thinking
can lead to a change of mood, premises without a trace
of joy can lead to a joyful conclusion:

> "But after wo I rede us to be merye,
>
> .   .   .   .   .   .
>
> I rede that we make of sorwes two
> O parfit joye, lastynge everemo."
>
> (I, 3068–72)

Chaucer uses animal imagery to the same end,
enriching and complicating the world by making
Theseus' positive qualities undermine the positive
qualities of Palamon and Arcite. The whole poem is
loaded with animal images that serve to endorse the
unbending courage and fierceness of Palamon and
Arcite. Particularly noticeable are the animal images
in the treatment of Emetreus and Lygurge. Yet right
after Chaucer describes in animal imagery the fighting of Palamon and Arcite, he has Theseus think of
the lion — the noblest and fiercest of animals and probably the most frequently cited one in the poem — as
an example of what a lord ought *not* to be:

> ... "Fy
> Upon a lord that wol have no mercy,
> But been a leon, bothe in word and dede."
>
> (I, 1773–75)

He associates the lion not only with lack of mercy but with lack of discretion and rationality. He goes on to ridicule the "jolitee" of the two cousins by saying that it puts Emelye in the position of a silly beast — "she woot namoore of al this hoote fare,/By God, than woot a cookow or an hare!"

Arcite and Palamon sometimes engage in what might look like thinking: making logical distinctions and drawing inferences (I, 1152–86, 1223–74, and in particular 1280–1333). But in every case they are using words and thoughts to vindicate a mood and point of view they already hold: anger and self-justification in the first case and despair in the other two. They use the ingredients of thought not for flexibility but for avoiding flexibility. Theseus is significant because he uses words and thoughts to arrive at a new mood and point of view, and thereby calls into question some things formerly taken for granted.

Saturn is the second main influence in the poem to deepen and enrich the world and thus transcend the *demande d'amour*. He stands in the same relation to Venus and Mars as Theseus does to Palamon and Arcite. In fact, Saturn gives the briefest statement of the dialectic at the heart of the poem — trying to end conflict and make peace between two opposing sides without destroying their essential opposition:

> "Bitwixe yow ther moot be som tyme pees,
> Al be ye noght of o compleccioun,
> That causeth al day swich divisioun."
>
> (I, 2474–76)

The awkward syntax here makes the last line reverberate: it is almost as though he implies that the difference in "complexion" between Mars and Venus
causes daily "divisions" in Nature. To the extent that
he brings peace to contrasting complexions in Nature,
he is exactly like the "faire cheyne of love" in its operation on the four elements.

Yet Saturn employs a remarkably violent method
for bringing peace and a remarkably disordered
method for bringing harmony. Not only does he kill
Arcite, but he does so by means of a frightening piece
of black chaos — Pluto's little monster that bursts out
of the ground. And Chaucer emphasizes chaos in showing that the malady that kills Arcite operates outside
nature:

> Hym gayneth neither....
> Vomyt upward, ne downward laxatif.
> Al is tobrosten thilke regioun;
> Nature hath now no dominacioun.

> (I, 2755–58)

Arcite has been swept beyond the realm of natural
law.[43] Saturn's description of himself (I, 2456 ff.)
also stresses the violent and chaotic.

Thus, though Saturn and Theseus are made
parallel by the poem's symmetrical structure, they are
also contrasted in such a way as to deepen the world
finally created in the poem. Theseus is associated with
order, structure, with a relenting mind and the sparing
of lives; Saturn is associated with chaos, violence, with
an unrelenting mind and the taking of lives.

Theseus' First-Mover speech is the third main in-

fluence for enriching and complicating the world so
that the *demande d'amour* is transcended rather than
straightforwardly answered. More than anything else
in the poem it confirms the sense that *neither* cousin
is the worthier, for the speech is a piece of reasoning
that both contains and transcends the conflict upon
which the whole poem is constructed: Palamon and
Venus versus Arcite and Mars. That is, the speech endorses elements centrally associated with Palamon and
Venus while it also endorses elements centrally associated with Arcite and Mars.

The links between the speech and Palamon-
Venus are clear. Most obvious, of course, is the fact
that the speech is on Palamon's behalf, as it were, and
gives him the prize: it unites him with the woman he
has sought all along. It achieves this through reasoning
linked with Palamon's sponsor, Venus: the speech
reiterates that the "faire cheyne of love" — the principle of attraction that holds together the primal elements of fire, air, water, and earth — is the most potent
force in the universe (I, 2987–93). This recalls the
earlier assertion, in the description of the temple of
Venus, that hers is the most powerful force there is:

> Thus may ye seen that wysdom ne richesse,
> Beautee ne sleighte, strengthe ne hardynesse,
> Ne may with Venus holde champartie,
> For as hir list the world than may she gye.
>
> (I, 1947–50)

Both the tone and the content of Theseus' speech reflect Palamon's quality of religious piety and humility.[44]

The links between the speech and Arcite-Mars are less obvious but are striking once noticed. First, there is the strong emphasis in the speech on death and dissolution, both associated with Mars. Furthermore, the speech reflects Arcite's characteristic stance in that it stands back and looks with perspective at the nature of things. Arcite said it was foolish to seek felicity as blindly as a drunk mouse (I, 1261 ff.), and here Theseus advocates the use of sober, farsighted intelligence in the pursuit of felicity. Arcite said it was foolish to strive for a bone like two dogs that allow an eagle to snatch the prize away from both (I, 1177 ff.), and here Theseus attempts to prevent an outcome in which both "hounds" lose the "bone." Arcite said that promises do not matter when it comes to love (I, 1164 ff.), and here Theseus maintains that from a cosmic perspective ("at the king's court" — in Jupiter's court) the living must realize such love and create such joy as the constricted nature of things permits. Even law and justice are not the highest priorities: where Arcite said that "therefore positif lawe and swich decree/Is broken alday for love in ech degree" (I, 1166–67), here Theseus says that vows should be set aside for the sake of love.

This final speech also effects, tonally, a reconciliation between sorrow and joy. It stresses equally that all things decay and pass away and yet that all living things renew themselves and beget new life:

> "He hath so wel biset his ordinaunce,
> That speces of thynges and progressiouns
> Shullen enduren by successiouns."

(I, 3012–14)

It also implies thereby a kind of reconciliation between growth and disorder or decay.[45]

In *The Knight's Tale* Chaucer asks a delicately balanced binary question — he poses a paradigm *demande d'amour*. But since the knights are equally worthy, the poem ends up testing the question or the genre more than it does the knights. It is unsatisfactory to say, merely, that it is a poem about how two men loved and deserved a woman equally. It is more accurate to say the poem explores so fully the conflict between two worthy men for a woman that it finally reveals profound limitations in the usual way of judging the worthiness of knights.[46] The poem thus reveals the limits of chivalry and courtly love. It moves from an immersion in the binary dispute to a perspective from which we see the limits of what at first appeared to be the whole world — "the litel spot of erthe that with the se embraced is" (in *Troilus*). There is a distancing that feels pagan, suggesting Anaximander:

It is necessary that things should pass away into that from which they are born. For they must pay one another the penalty and compensation for their mutual injustice in the order of time. (DK13B1 = KR112)

As a general intuitive reading suggests, the poem moves from a static, symmetrical opposition to a state of complex, paradoxical process. The original opposition is embodied in the neat question of love between Palamon and Arcite, and the final process is symbolized in Theseus' changes of mind: from sternness to mercy, from death to life, from sorrow to joy. There is a sense, finally, that *neither* cousin is really worthy until he enters this more complex world: a world where suffering and death are more fully experienced, and a world more complex because it contains the interactions between contraries that Theseus embodies.

THE OPPOSITION at the heart of *The Nun's Priest's Tale* is a question of exegesis: does Chauntecleer's dream foretell the future or not? He believes that it does and piles up massive authority to support his interpretation. But Pertelote argues that it is just something he ate and prescribes a laxative and an emetic. This question of exegesis is the center of an opposition that polarizes all the important elements of the poem.

Chauntecleer explains the dream in terms of its meaning; Pertelote explains it in terms of its cause. He looks to the future; his wife looks to the past. He emphasizes the mind and spirit; she emphasizes the body. He is, quite literally, imaginative and a dreamer, for in his dream he sees images not produced by his senses and finds truths in these dream images that he could not find in his senses or even in logic; she is a pragmatic materialist.

In emphasizing the meaning rather than the cause of events, Chauntecleer asserts his connection with distant times, places, and people. He sees himself participating in a process with men of all eras and learning from their example. These meanings even connect him with different planes of reality, for his explanation is ultimately religious: God put the world together in such a way that events can be signs of each other. Pertelote's response is simply that red choler causes dreams with red in them and melancholic humors cause dreams with black in them (VII, 2926–36). When she empties his dream images of meaning and sees there only clues to physical cause, she takes the role, as it were, of the empirical positivist.

Although she cites Cato and displays what a modern reader might feel as recondite, bookish medical lore, there is really an implicit contrast between Chauntecleer's reiterated appeal to authority and Pertelote's to experience.[47] She appeals to operational, physical cause-and-effect, and to what contemporary readers would have perceived as a roll-up-your-sleeves science. She reinforces her empirical stance by using physical terms for emotional and characterological states: "Have ye no mannes herte, and han a berd?" (VII, 2920). Chauntecleer, on the other hand, cites bookish authority from every corner of the library: English history, Greek history and literature, Roman history and literature, and the Old and New Testaments. Moreover, his appeal is to the past, while hers — in spite of the ancient roots of humoral medicine — is to the present.

Chaucer renders in Chauntecleer's voice the sounds and rhythms of the pedant:

> "Madame," quod he, "graunt mercy of youre loore.
> But nathelees, as touchyng daun Catoun,
> That hath of wysdom swich a greet renoun,
> Though that he bad no dremes for to drede . . ."
>
> (VII, 2970–73)

His speech sounds the note of the intellectual's fastidious qualifier — the prudent hedge that tries to ensure irrefutability:

> "Reed eek of Joseph, and ther shul ye see
> Wher dremes be *somtyme* — *I sey nat alle* —
> Warnynge of thynges that shul after falle."
>
> (VII, 3130–32; emphasis added)

This distinction between his emphasis on meaning and hers on cause — his on authority and hers on experience — ultimately implies a contrast between two different kinds of knowing. Her kind of knowing leads to action. She sees a disequilibrium among his humors — a defective homeostatic system — and she sets about correcting it through a definite plan of physical therapy. She has a clear model of what is supposed to happen. His kind of knowing, on the other hand, leads to no action at all; it is knowledge for its own sake. He settles for insight. Although he says,

> "Shortly I seye, as for conclusioun,
> That I shal han of this avisioun
> Adversitee;"
>
> (VII, 3151–53)

he does nothing at all about it.

Yet in a sense, though his words and thoughts lead to no action, he takes his knowledge more seriously than she does hers. Perhaps because he deals only in knowledge, not in action, knowledge itself means more to him. Anyway, he cannot bear to be contradicted. In order to save his hypothesis, he produces an elaborate, gothic structure of argument.

The opposition is more precisely one between their cognitive and rhetorical styles. He builds elaborate verbal structures; she cuts things down, takes the hot air out. Indeed, she sees "fumes" and "hot humours" as part of his trouble (VII, 2924, 2957). Where he takes everything intensely seriously, she characteristically debunks:

> "Nothyng, God woot, but vanitee in sweven is."
>
> (VII, 2922)

> "Be myrie, housbonde, for youre fader kyn!
> Dredeth no dreem."
>
> (VII, 2968–69)

The obvious interpretation of the poem is true enough: Chauntecleer's vanity overcomes his instinctive fear of a fox.

> For natureely a beest desireth flee
> Fro his contrarie, if that he may it see,
> Though he never erst hadde seyn it with his ye.
>
> (VII, 3279–81)

But the medium for his vanity is *language*. His eyes tell him to flee, but once he listens with his ears, he is in trouble:

> . . . whan he gan hym espye,
> He wolde han fled, but that the fox anon
> Seyde, "Gentil sire . . ."
>
> (VII, 3282–84)

It is words and thoughts that drown his vision's instinctive promptings. His vanity operates through his ability, quite literally, to rationalize. Only a creative head full of words and thoughts could believe the fox is after music. But it is also his creativity — unexpected and more than instinctive — that permits him finally to escape from the fox's jaws. This creativity works through his gift for speaking under any and all circumstances. Instinct at the critical moment would lead to great fear and panic, but in fact Chauntecleer comes up with brazen verbal ingenuity. The fox is tricked, not by a subtle plan, but by the unexpectedness of even the simplest verbal guile under those circumstances. Pertelote, of course, has no difficulty doing what instinct prompts, and she runs away as soon as she sees the fox.

To his wife's skeptical natural scientist he is both bookish scholar and creative artist. The medieval concept of rhetorician-rhetor-rhetoric combines without differentiation the roles of scholar and artist.[48] His crowing, like his father's, is high and splendid art — like the church organ on mass days. Both he and the narrator conceive his whole identity and function in terms of this artistic — and sexual — creativity.

It is characteristic of Chauntecleer as artist and crower to stretch away from the earth:

> This Chauntecleer stood hye upon his toos,
> Strecchynge his nekke, and heeld his eyen cloos,
> And gan to crowe loude for the nones.
>
> (VII, 3331–33)

He is diffident about full commerce with the ground:

> He looketh as it were a grym leoun,
> And on his toos he rometh up and doun;
> Hym deigned nat to sette his foot to grounde.
>
> (VII, 3179–81)

Things that are high both in stature and in location are needed to describe him: a church organ, an abbey clock, castle battlements, burnished gold. He is royal, a lion, an angel. For his crowing he stays in touch with the sun and the planets and the equinoctial circles, and he always knows the degrees of heaven. He is the earthling whose job it is to bring the message of the heavens. His bookishness is part of his disdain for lowly, common, down-to-earth things. He crows with his eyes closed, and his vision comes in a dream when his eyes are closed. He does not heed the common physical world through his senses. Though he sees the fox, he is functionally blind to him — just as in *The Merchant's Tale* (IV, 2354 ff.), January was functionally blind to what must have been the striking sight of his wife and her friend in the tree above him. Chauntecleer is blind, in short, to basic, common physical things. Even his verbal style is a species of leaving the ground: it is no accident that phrases like "rhetorical flight" or "getting carried away" are used for his kind of utterance. His getting lost in digressions is like losing contact with the ground. Even his extraordinary sexual activity can be seen as a special capacity for soaring.

Pertelote, on the other hand, is concerned with down-to-earth things like worms, herbs, digestion, laxatives, and emetics. She lies down to bathe in the sand. She tries to get Chauntecleer to bend down and pick up lowly things from the ground to eat. We sense in her a gift for keeping her eyes open and not losing contact with the empirical world. She keeps her feet on the ground.

Behind everything else, of course, is an opposition of gender, especially with respect to language. The two other males in the poem, the fox and the narrator, share Chauntecleer's complex verbal qualities. The narrator, like Chauntecleer, makes impassioned rhetorical flights — verbal songs, really — and gets carried away by the feelings involved and engendered (VII, 3226 ff.). He also loves learned allusion, just as Chauntecleer does (VII, 3212, 3227, 3312). Both make long speeches and tend to lose themselves in digressions. The fox, the third male, also winds Chauntecleer to him by a virtuoso verbal performance. He "charms" in the root sense.[49] Like Chauntecleer, he is tricked out of his instincts, out of his dinner, because of his weakness for words: he cannot resist listening to Chauntecleer nor making a vaunting speech back to his pursuers. All three males invest themselves heavily in words and can be said to make music with their voices. Pertelote, on the other hand, though she is not wordless like her fellow wives, clearly does not make an art form of words as the males do. She is operational and pragmatic in the linguistic sphere as in most others.[50] Notice how Chaucer even suggests the tone of the maternal cluck in Pertelote's solicitous advice:

> "I shal myself to herbes techen yow
> That shul been for youre hele and for youre prow.
>
> .   .   .   .   .   .
>
> To purge yow bynethe and eek above.
> Foryet nat this, for Goddes owene love!
> Ye been ful coleryk of compleccioun;
>
> .   .   .   .   .   .
>
> Of herbe yve, growyng in oure yeerd, ther mery is;
> Pekke hem up right as they growe and ete hem yn."
>
> (VII, 2949–67)

Perhaps the reader will object here that Chaucer has built an ironic contrast only between humans and animals, and I am twisting it into a battle of the sexes. Of course, there is an ironic contrast between humans and animals: the joke is that though the animals are so verbal and polymath, the complete language production of humans in the poem is "Out! harrow! . . . weylaway!/Ha! Ha! the fox!" (VII, 3380–81). Humans seem to emit nothing but clucks and quacks:

> Of bras they broghten bemes, and of box,
> Of horn, of boon, in whiche they blewe and powped,
> And therwithal they skriked and they howped.
>
> (VII, 3398–3400)

Furthermore, almost all the animals have names; none of the humans does.

But on the other hand, the opposition is not only, and perhaps not even primarily, one between humans and animals. The creatures in the tale's "human frame" — *i. e.,* the widow's household — are not in fact all humans. But they are all females: a widow, two daughters, three sows, three cows, and a sheep named Malle.

Chaucer can scarcely refrain from writing about marriage and the battle of the sexes whatever the ostensible subject of a poem. He often makes asides about women. A good example occurs when the narrator blames all this disaster on a woman's advice — and then hastily takes it back; he was just kidding:

> Wommennes conseils been ful ofte colde;
> Wommennes conseil broghte us first to wo.
> And made Adam fro Paradys to go,
> Ther as he was ful myrie and wel at ese.
> But for I noot to whom it myght displese,
> If I conseil of wommen wolde blame,
> Passe over, for I seyde it in my game.
> Rede auctours, where they trete of swich mateere,
> And what they seyn of wommen ye may heere.
> Thise been the cokkes wordes, and nat myne;
> I kan noon harm of no womman divyne.
>
> (VII, 3256–66)

Chaucer follows nature and grants color to the male. The description of Chauntecleer is a passage often cited to illustrate not merely Chaucer's use of vivid color, but also Chaucer's use of "rhetorical colors" in general. Chaucer and the rhetorical handbooks refer to skill in poetry as possession of "colors." The fox too is described in the dream as brightly colored. And the fox and the narrator follow Chaun-

tecleer in using the full range of rhetorical colors in
their speech.

The opposite qualities are associated with the females in the poem. Everything about the widow and
her household is a denial of color:

> No wyn ne drank she, neither whit ne reed;
>
> > (VII, 2842)
>
> Of poynaunt sauce hir neded never a deel.
>
> > (VII, 2834)

Black and white and dullness are emphasized:

> Ful sooty was hire bour and eek hir halle,
>
> > (VII, 2832)
>
> Hir bord was served moost with whit and blak, —
> Milk and broun breed.
>
> > (VII, 2843–44)

In Pertelote there is not such a literal absence of color.
We are told that she was colored like her husband, that
she was fair about her throat. And also, to startle us
comically when we have forgotten we are listening
to animals, that the redness of her eyes was beautiful
and sexually exciting. But clearly Chaucer makes
Chauntecleer outshine her in color.[51]

I cannot resist schematizing this opposition to
show not only how completely it pervades the poem
but also how Chaucer polarizes here so many of our
most basic categories: male/female; mind/body;
words/action; authority/experience; the learned and

creative artist/the empirical pragmatist; building up elaborate structures/cutting things down; color/colorlessness; stretching up away from the earth/bending down toward the earth.

Chaucer builds this rich opposition only to transcend it. Just as in *The Knight's Tale,* where the problem was the problem, the *demande d'amour,* so here too the problem is the polar, marital, exegetical dispute itself. The question — "Is Chauntecleer or Pertelote correct about the dream?" — cannot be straightforwardly answered. Even though their responses contradict each other, both are correct.

Chauntecleer is right that his dream is true, and Pertelote is wrong to deny it. But this is not a satisfactory account of the poem. Chaucer shows ironically through mock-heroic that a person's knowledge consists in what he *does* as much as in what he says: by adding language to the animal world, the poem shows more pointedly than ever how misleading it is to identify knowledge only with what is said in language. Chauntecleer's "answer" — in the fullness that Chaucer shows it — is right only at the level of words.

First of all, the very qualities that gave him the right verbal answer — his tendencies to see meanings, trust words, and ride both on long flights — are the same qualities that prevent him from benefiting from the dream. The moment he began to listen to the fox's words, he no longer felt the danger the dream warned him of.

These same qualities also explain why he did nothing beforehand about the very danger he argued was coming. The sequence of events makes the point: right after his interminable defense of the truth of his dream (when he "defies" laxatives with a crash), rather than take any precaution, he flies down from his perch, feathers his wife twenty times, starts in on his other wives, and begins to eat. His intellectuality blinds him to how much he is a creature of appetites, or at least he fails to integrate his "animality" into his serious awareness and conscious thinking. He simply does not see that the morning's sexuality and eating deny everything for which he has just argued.

The narrator speaks as though Chauntecleer were persuaded by his wife.

> My tale is of a cok ...
> That tok his conseil of his wyf, with sorwe.
>
> (VII, 3252–53)

But of course nothing of the sort takes place. The narrator shares Chauntecleer's male tendency to see an event as the consequence of words and meanings when it is really an instance of physical causation. What he calls "taking counsel" or implies to be persuasion is really a physical matter of Chauntecleer seeing her body in the lightening dawn and simply forgetting about the exegetical dispute. And similarly, in Chauntecleer's dealings with the fox, appetite goes under the name of rational discourse.

Thus, the initial, structural question of the poem

— how seriously to take the truth of Chauntecleer's dream — must be given a paradoxical, double answer. Chauntecleer is correct to interpret it as he does, but he is also incorrect because his very capacity to come up with the right answer involves blind spots which lead to the wrong behavior. If Pertelote had such a dream, she would not get in trouble. But at the same time her gift for the right behavior produces the wrong verbal answer.

As a little emblem, analogous to the way Chaucer affirms the two contradictory interpretations of the dream, nothing could be more elegant than Chauntecleer's interpretation of a Latin text for his wife:

> "For al so siker as *in principio,*
> *Mulier est hominis confusio,* —
> Madame, the sentence of this Latyn is,
> 'Womman is mannes joye and al his blis.' "
>
> (VII, 3163–66)

His interpretation of the Latin is at once exactly wrong and exactly right: wrong, obviously, as a mistranslation; right, however, as the essential explication of *why* woman is man's confusion. It is left fittingly ambiguous as to whether the mistranslation is a case of the pedant's compliment involving a private and condescending irony or whether the mistranslation is itself an instance of the confusion that women cause.[52] At any rate, this dialectical exegesis echoes that of the dream in that here too the finesse turns on language, learning, and the difference between the sexes.

The Nun's Priest's Tale is probably a late work, and it seems a touchstone for what is most essentially Chaucerian in Chaucer's poetry. I think that I can show how something special is involved when Chaucer makes Chauntecleer and Pertelote equally right about the dream — more than is involved, for example, in making Palamon and Arcite equally worthy of Emelye. What is special stems from a crucial analogy between Chauntecleer's dream and the poem as a whole. Both are objects of exegesis, and both invite the same exegetical question of how *seriously* to take them. Should we — with the poem as with the dream — inflate and read in all manner of intensely serious meanings, or should we cut things down and not be carried away, not stand for any nonsense? This question is raised about the whole poem most explicitly in the Nun's Priest's concluding words. He allegedly answers the question by exhorting us to take the poem as serious doctrine, but actually he intensifies the question because his words are so lamely tacked on at the end and represent such an unconvincing change of tone:[53]

> But ye that holden this tale a folye,
> As of a fox, or of a cok and hen,
> Taketh the moralite, goode men.
> For seint Paul seith that al that writen is,
> To oure doctrine it is ywrite, ywis;
> Taketh the fruyt, and lat the chaf be stille.
>
> (VII, 3438–43)

This analogy between a dream and a narrative poem is central to medieval poetry and to Chaucer —

most obviously in his early poems. In *The Parlement of Foules,* for example, the poem *is* a dream: it consists simultaneously of narrative and revelation. So too, *The Romaunt of the Rose.* Indeed, all of Chaucer's early poetry implies a convergence of the questions of how to interpret a dream and how to interpret a narrative poem.[54]

Chauntecleer's dream and the poem as a whole are analogous not just because they are both objects of exegesis. They are linked by a whole complex of qualities associated with Chauntecleer and with the medieval concept of rhetoric: dream, vision, fantasy, narrative, poetry, color, ornament, and elaborate structure.[55] Chauntecleer is the source both of dreams and of extravagant rhetoric like the poem. Rhetoric in the Middle Ages implied both narrative and argument, two aspects of the single art of making words have the desired effect upon an audience. The *art of rhetoric* and the *art of poetry* were nearly interchangeable terms. Here Chauntecleer, like other medieval poets, switches back and forth, almost without noticing, between argument and narrative.[56]

Thus the two questions — how seriously to take the dream and how seriously to take the poem — are really the same question: how seriously to take that complex of qualities associated with Chauntecleer and with rhetoric that are, in the poem's terms, the vapors of the male imagination, the male impulse to rise, to move away from the earth, to soar. The question gets the same double answer: just as Chaucer both ridicules and endorses Chauntecleer's exegesis of his dream, he both ridicules and endorses these qualities. To do this, he uses the same strategy he used in *Troilus and Criseyde:* he makes the reader say yes, no, and then yes again, to end up believing in both.

The first step in the process, the initial *yes,* is truncated in this broadly ironic work. If irony is broad enough, it may approach sarcasm, in which there is virtually no double-take or reversal in the reader's response to the words. But though the initial, serious *yes* may be truncated here, it certainly occurs for some readers. I know that I am not alone when I seriously assent to the straightforward power of some of the high rhetoric of the poem. At the moment of reading, I am naively moved, for example, by some of the images and comparisons in the initial description of Chauntecleer and Pertelote, and by certain of the more intense, extended rhythms in Chauntecleer's and the narrator's flights of epic rhetoric.

But the ironic response, the *no,* predominates. The qualities associated with Chauntecleer and rhetoric are made ridiculous in countless ways. Chauntecleer is consistently more foolish than his wife. His hypothesis about his dream may be theoretically correct, but only the event makes one believe it: her presentation is persuasive while his is windily absurd.

Chaucer invites the reader to see the ridiculousness of high rhetoric by means of ironically timed juxtapositions. Chauntecleer's flight down from their perch to feather his wife twenty times deflates the long, serious rhetoric which precedes it. The narrator's inflated rhetoric is similarly punctured, as when his heavy attempt at theological philosophy ends with "I wol nat han to do of swich mateere;/My tale is of a cok." (VII, 3251–52). His loftier epic comparison of the barnyard catastrophe to ancient tragedies, including that of Troy, is sharply punctuated by raucous quacking, hooting, and pooping. In each case we have a comic burst of physicality, which pricks the bubble of inflated rhetoric slowly and carefully built up. The "humble widow" black-and-white frame serves the same purpose for this splendidly colored narrative. All these mock-heroic contrasts jolt us back to the physical facts of life: these are silly, trivial, barnyard animals strutting on dung. Tiny details of imagery jolt us with animality in the same way after we have forgotten that we are listening to chickens (e. g., VII, 2866, 3161, 3169, 3267).

In all these ways serious rhetoric is ridiculed. It is foolish to try to raise the seriousness and dignity of events by describing them in language pumped full of color, bookish allusion, extra meaning, and fancy structure. The reader answers no to the question of whether to take seriously the complex of qualities associated with Chauntecleer and rhetoric.

But this mock-epic aspect of the poem, however powerful, is only part of it. A third and affirming response occurs — "straight," serious, but wholly non-naive — over against the earlier naive and ironic responses. For the *way* the poem pokes fun at Chauntecleer's and the narrator's verbal inflation is through *Chaucer's* use of fancy rhetoric. To make fun of the vapors of the male imagination, Chaucer himself exploits them so brilliantly that the final effect of the whole performance is a *celebration* of the very virtuoso rhetoric that is debunked: imagination, words, digression, excess, self-seriousness, learning, and intellectual subtlety.

But this celebration is interestingly reticent. The point that the poem makes most powerfully — and it must express one of Chaucer's deepest convictions — is one that is least stated: to put events into words as full as possible of color, dignity, and extra meaning is as important an activity as humans can engage in. Usually Chaucer implies the opposite: poetry is just a way to pass the time of day, just a joke that really means very little.

This three-stage procedure, with its final reticence, may sound elaborate, but it is a common, instinctive strategy in everyday utterance; and it works. The speaker puts in joking terms what he is reluctant to say openly. He wants to say it but he wants just as strongly not to say it — or in this case to say the opposite. So he achieves his goal by seeming to devote himself to making fun of it. Under the cover of not meaning it, he gets the idea firmly into the listener's mind.

Thus the binary question raised by the dream is the same one raised by the poem itself: what are we to make of the elaborate, "phantastic," and often silly creations of the imagination — dreams, stories, intricate and playful arrangements of words? All the elements in the poem serve to enforce and uphold opposite answers. On the one hand, it is absurd to take them seriously. To do so blinds us to humbler, concrete, and very important aspects of physical reality — notably sex and death. But on the other hand, the poem implies that if we do not take seriously the fumes of the imagination, we ignore our highest capacity. To achieve not just beauty and pleasure but even truth, we must sometimes risk precarious bubbles of imaginative creation and extravagant flights of inference.

V. FREEDOM AND NECESSITY IN CHAUCER

THE PROBLEM of freedom and necessity is central in *Troilus and Criseyde*, as I tried to demonstrate in Chapter II; but when a poet is deeply concerned with an issue, he writes of it continually. The tongue returns to the aching tooth. Chaucer's treatment of freedom and necessity takes diverse forms.

The Knight's Tale in general and the opposition between Palamon and Arcite in particular carry an implied opposition between freedom and necessity. Palamon is a bit more passive, immersed, helpless; Arcite is a bit more detached and tough-minded, taking agency more into his own hands. With respect to the whole tale, the behavior of the characters seems free enough, but a sense of fate is strong too. The humans are so overshadowed by all the machinery of the planets and the gods that their wills seem unimportant, though not visibly hampered. The language dwells incessantly upon prison and prison imagery. Even when Arcite gets out of the prison, so constantly evoked in Part I, he calls his new state more prisonlike than the old one. The temple of Mars is like a dungeon.[57]

Theseus' final speech transcends this opposition between freedom and necessity. First of all, it asserts necessity strongly throughout — more strongly, in fact, than any other part of the poem. Theseus even intensifies the prison imagery:

> ". . . [W]hy have we hevynesse,
> That goode Arcite . . .
> Departed is . . .
> Out of this foule prisoun of this lyf?"
>
> (I, 3058–61)

The message of the speech is that the First Mover has established things according to bonds and bounds, and that a man who strives against these decrees is a rebel and a willful fool (I, 3005, 3044, 3045, 3057). And yet the "conclusioun" that Theseus draws from his "long serye" is a strong exhortation to avoid passivity and to assert agency. He tells Palamon and Emelye not to give in, not to follow their vows, not even to follow their feelings, but instead willfully and freely to *make* happiness for themselves out of their sorrow. Theseus condenses this dialectical resolution of necessity and freedom into a line Chaucer remained fond of: "To maken vertu of necessitee" (I, 3042). Note the Middle English senses of "vertu": not just abstract "principle" but active "force" and "strength," almost "agency" itself. The line is an oxymoron: it proclaims necessity but exhorts free action. Chaucer's handling of Boccaccio underlines this sense of proclaiming freedom in the teeth of necessity. In Boccaccio the happy ending is presented as a gift of fickle fortune, but Chaucer departs from his source to make it the result of conscious decision and agency.

Theseus is really saying something very practical. Because Palamon and Arcite did not fully see and accept necessity, notwithstanding a few resigned pronouncements by Arcite, they lacked real freedom. Because Theseus truly sees and accepts necessity, he can achieve greater freedom and agency, and can help Palamon and Emelye to do the same. Trying to get away from what is inevitable makes you unfree. About this fact of human experience "ther nedeth noght noon auctoritee t'allegge,/For it is preeved by experience" (I, 3000–1).

The Nun's Priest's Tale is an elegant treatment of both the general problem of freedom and necessity and of the special problem of free will and foreknowledge. Here Chaucer is a playful, sophisticated virtuoso, enjoying the mastery of what he feels deeply and has bought with serious labor in the two earlier poems, *Troilus and Criseyde* and *The Knight's Tale*.

It is like Chaucer to embody this virtuosity in the narrator's befuddlement. The narrator drags in his little speech about freedom and necessity and then drops the issue gracelessly and ineffectually (VII, 3230–52), as though startled to realize he has wandered into something totally irrelevant. And with respect to the surface texture, the speech feels like an unrelated digression, a little rhetorical set-piece out of the handbooks, like the one about Friday being a tragic day of the week.

Here is how the narrator sets out the problem:

> O Chauntecleer, acursed be that morwe
> That thou into that yerd flaugh fro the bemes!

Thou were ful wel ywarned by thy dremes
That thilke day was perilous to thee;
But what that God forwoot moot nedes bee,
After the opinioun of certein clerkis.

(VII, 3230–35)

Though he goes on to waffle about whether or not he really believes these scholars, he clearly sees the problem as a conflict between Chauntecleer's freedom and God's constraining foreknowledge.

What the narrator does not see — and what Chaucer thereby disguises — is that what looks like a conflict is really an analogy: the poem builds a *parallel* between Chauntecleer's "warning" and God's "forwooting." Foreknowers have been proliferated. Both Chauntecleer and God have foreknowledge of this future event through a piece of special, out-of-time, nonrational, nondiscursive knowledge, and there is thus an essential analogy between Chauntecleer and God as foreknowers.

The piquancy that comes from making Chauntecleer like God is characteristic of this mock-heroic poem: the *reductio ad absurdum* of making a rooster so smart. He is, indeed, lordly in his dominion over his chicken-yard universe. His qualities of mind and spirit — and masculine creativity — are comic analogies to God.

I think we can even take a phrase that has proved vexing to commentators — the third line of the following passage — as reinforcing this analogy between Chauntecleer and God:

> A col-fox ful of sly iniquitee,
> That in the grove hadde woned yeres three,
> By heigh ymaginacioun forncast,
> The same nyght . . .

(VII, 3215–18)

Baugh's footnote sets out the difficulties very clearly and then stops on the brink of the solution:

The interpretation of this line is uncertain. Manly takes it to mean "predestined by divine foresight," Robinson "by divine foreknowledge," and Tatlock "by decree of almighty Providence." This makes acceptable sense, but it must be admitted that there is no other instance (in Chaucer or in the *NED*) of *heigh ymaginacioun* used in this sense and the interpretation strains somewhat the most common meaning of *forncast*. Sisam, on the other hand, in his edition of the tale (Oxford, 1927) translates " 'foreseen by the exalted imagination' — referring to Chauntecleer's dream," and this interpretation is supported by V. M. Hamm (*MLN*, LXIX. 394–5), who traces the association of the imagination with prophetic vision through dreams back to Plato and points out that Chaucer's phrase has its closest parallel in Dante's *alta fantasia*. Taking the line to refer to Chauntecleer's dream puts the least strain on *forncast*.[58]

The difficulties disappear when we realize that the line refers to both: to Chauntecleer's knowledge of the future (his dream and his correct exegesis) and also, by analogy, to God's foreknowledge.

The narrator thus asks his question in a wrong-headed way that ensures befuddlement. He says, in effect, "If only we understood the problem of God's foreknowledge, then we could understand this story." If he turned things upside down, he would have a fruitful question: "If only we worked out our understanding of this story, then we could finally understand the problem of God's foreknowledge."[59] Where Boethius in *Consolation* V solves the problem of foreknowledge by carefully analyzing different kinds of knowledge — by epistemology — Chaucer uses a comically apt thought-experiment. He shows us foreknowledge in action — Chauntecleer's.

The narrator poses the question carefully in terms of God's foreknowledge:

> But I ne kan nat bulte it to the bren
> As kan the hooly doctour Augustyn,
> Or Boece, or the Bisshop Bradwardyn,
> [1] Wheither that Goddes worthy forwityng
> Streyneth me nedely for to doon a thyng, —
> "nedely" clepe I *symple necessitee;*
> [2] Or elles, if *free choys* be grounted me
> To do that same thyng, or do it noght,
> Though God forwoot it er that was wroght;
> [3] Or if his wityng streyneth never a deel
> But by *necessitee condicioneel.*
> I wol nat han to do of swich mateere;
> My tale is of a cok, as ye may heere,
> That tok his conseil of his wyf, with sorwe.
> (VII, 3240–53; emphasis and numbers added)

Chauntecleer's dream knowledge produces all three conditions. "Free choys": it warns him of something he could avoid. "Symple necessitee": the very qualities that give him this special knowledge lead him into the fox's jaws. Yet the very fact that it leads to both at once constitutes "necessitee condicioneel." But what Chaucer shows most concerning Chauntecleer's dream is what Boethius demonstrates about God's foreknowledge: the knowledge of an event is different from its cause. Chauntecleer's knowledge, in itself, does *not* cause the event (despite the psychological link between the qualities that help him read the dream and the qualities that lead him into the fox's jaws). Nor, however, does the dream knowledge free him from the event. Chauntecleer's dream knowledge illustrates God's special knowledge: neither can be said to hamper free behavior or in any way box in normal reality. It is all a matter of what the knower might *do* with such knowledge.

Thus the foreknowledge problem, which is epistemological and analytic, leads to the broader one of general human freedom and necessity. Chauntecleer is both free and unfree. He is free in that he certainly cannot blame what happened on anyone but himself — not on God, his wife, or the fox (the narrator notwithstanding). He was warned. He "did" what "happened to him." Yet he is unfree in that his behavior seems inevitable from the way his mind works.

Which is the free one, Chauntecleer or Pertelote? Clearly he is. His predilection for language and thought frees him from instinct, from a single, rigid, programmed, or wired-in response to a fox. On the other hand, even though Pertelote's entire repertoire in the presence of a fox is only one behavior, Chaucer gives a sense of what a delightful freedom it is to let instinct — *i. e.,* convention and history — determine one's response to the environment.

Finally, Chaucer deepens the sense of simultaneous freedom and necessity by his use of animals. If such a silly animal is so free and yet so deluded in his pretensions, what about us featherless bipeds with our sense of greater freedom and our tendency nevertheless to blame events on things outside ourselves? Thus mock-heroic deepens the paradox about freedom and necessity:

> "Now God," quod he, "my swevene recche aright,
> And kepe my body out of foul prisoun!
> Me mette how that I romed up and doun
> Withinne our yeerd, wheer as I saugh a beest."
>
> (VII, 2896–99)

What splendidly blind pretension to pray for God to keep him out of "foul prisoun" — using Theseus' words and Boethius' concept — when his very next words emphasize that he already lives in one. His whole universe is a little chicken yard, covered with dung and dust, presumably fenced, and he is totally dependent on a poverty-stricken widow.

The problem of marriage in Chaucer is really another working out of the problem of freedom and necessity. The question is, which member has "maistrie": how are freedom and necessity distributed between spouses?

The traditional or formalist side of Chaucer assigns "maistrie" to the husband. The universe is a hierarchy of authority, a great chain of command. Any breach is unnatural and wrong. The husband's "maistre" over his wife is analogous to God's over man, the religious or lay ruler's over his subject, and man's over animals. If the husband does not maintain his proper and traditional "maistrie," he is violating the true order of things and contributing to a breakdown of nature and society. According to this formalist view, it is the wife's role to submit or bear. (Note the common origin of the words *bear, burden, birth,* and *fertile.*) This is the view implied in Chaucer's satire of a foolish, weak husband and in his pious tales which celebrate the "patience" — the bearing rather than the doing — of the woman.

It is this idea of the man's natural *"maistrie"* that helps make Criseyde hesitate:

> "I am myn owene womman, wel at ese,
>
> .   .   .   .   .   .
>
> Right yong, and stonde unteyd in lusty leese,
>
> .   .   .   .   .   .
>
> Shal noon housbonde seyn to me 'chek mat!'
> . . . Allas! syn I am free,
> Sholde I now love, and put in jupartie
> My sikernesse, and thrallen libertee?"

(II, 750–73)

But just as Criseyde does not readily consent to the great chain of hierarchy, so too we find in Chaucer the opposite point of view about the relationship between the sexes: "maistrie" belongs to the woman. This view carries an empiricist, naturalist mood which says, in effect, "The hierarchical theory of the male 'maistrie' is all very well, but in real life, the woman always rules." This view associates the woman with Aristotle's model of God as the unmoved mover. The Miller makes the analogy explicit:

> "An housbonde shal nat been inquisityf
> Of Goddes pryvetee, nor of his wyf.
> So he may fynde Goddes foyson there."
>
> (I, 3163–65)

Her "pryvetee" is her "foyson" or plenty. As the unmoved mover, she is the cause of motion in others even though she does not move and is not moved; she is the empty plenitude. We get in *The Merchant's Tale* and *The Nun's Priest's Tale,* for example, the pagan, empirical sense of all the green forces in nature contributing to the inevitable "maistrie" of the wife (*e. g.,* January blindly embracing the tree in the garden as though trying to hold onto Nature herself). Those tales communicate a benign, detached, contemplative sense that this is the way Nature works.

In these two opposite conceptions of "maistrie" in marriage, one side implies that Nature operates through the husband as a vessel of order, form, and structure. The other side implies that Nature operates through the wife as a vessel of limitless energy, renewal, and fecundity.

Chaucer implies both views in his various renderings of love. The crudest, most baldly pragmatic version — such as the Miller would see — has it that the husband's only hope for a shred of his proper "maistrie" is to give it all to his wife quickly. Before she takes it. A less reductive version says that the husband's best response to the wife's "maistrie" is to overwhelm her with a free and generous gift of whatever "maistrie" he has, so as to inspire *her* to want to give up hers. The highest, nonpragmatic version — courtly and religious love — which is often Chaucer's most deeply felt poetry, says that the behavior that most fulfills the "vertu" of persons with "maistrie" — that most fulfills their potentiality, as the oak fulfills the acorn's — is to *submit* to anyone over whom they have authority. "The servant of the servant" is one of Chaucer's central ideas. Chaucer's treatments of love, in short, imply that "maistrie" need not rest in one or the other but rather in both. It is another way of showing how human life is simultaneously free and determined.

Two of Chaucer's most important words, "gentilesse" and "curteisye," almost always evoke this paradoxical idea of love in which "maistrie" resides in both-and-neither. This theme is summed up in *The Franklin's Tale* about "gentilesse." It is a story about people getting tangled up in one another and then getting untangled by each relinquishing his own "maistrie."

Christ is the archetypal lover who gives His own natural and proper "maistrie" to His subjects: He is the servant of His servants. Though the tales of Pa-

tient Griselda and Constance naturally bring to mind
the Virgin, Christ is the closer analogue. Those tales
get their power by telescoping two themes: that the
woman is below and therefore ought to submit to the
man, but also that it is the *wife* who has natural
"maistrie" and *because* of that she ought to give it up.
We miss the point by saying only that Griselda gets all
these troubles *in spite of* her goodness. Her husband
maltreats her *because* she is good: her goodness asks
for it, her character generates the events of the story.
But we also miss the point if we simply say that her
saccharine piety is an infuriating invitation to abuse.
Chaucer is not showing interpersonal perversity so
much as a religious image of nature: it is the "vertu"
of transcendent goodness to submit to a transcendent
degree. Griselda's goodness and her bearing/suffering
/patience, like Christ's, are linked with an implicit,
primal authority.

In this light Chaucer's seemingly absurd *envoi*
makes sense. Where the tale seems to celebrate patient
bearing, the *envoi* tells women not to bear things pa-
tiently. The contradiction invites the reader to stumble
over the otherwise quiet implication that such abject
passivity may embody natural "maistrie."

Wherever in Chaucer persons relinquish what is
rightfully theirs or bear suffering out of proportion to
what they deserve, it tends to be a sign of this paradoxical point of view about love and "maistrie." Magic
too is often a sign of it: things change miraculously
when someone attains this sort of love. *The Wife of
Bath's Tale* ends with the archetypal instance. The

tyrannical loathly lady becomes young, beautiful, and submissive when kissed by a lover who yields "maistrie." The magic transformations in nature that are central to the plot of *The Franklin's Tale* are also fraught with the theme that "maistrie" can manage somehow to reside in both the man and the woman and in neither. In short, Chaucer renders again, in his treatment of love and marriage, his perception of the human condition as simultaneously free and bound.

Chaucer's treatment of himself as a poet in relation to his sources is yet another way of transcending the opposition between freedom and necessity. Is he free and fully responsible for what he writes, or does he lack freedom through a poetic bondage to his sources?

The first verdict is that he lacks freedom. His most frequent message is, in effect, "Who me? It wasn't I who said those things!" He repeatedly insists that he writes only what his source contains, and only changes a word here and there (*e. g., Troilus and Criseyde* III, 1324–36; *Tales,* VII, 943–66). He likes to cite his "author," and the word still carried strong connotations of "authority." He says he has to follow his authority because he has no *experience* of his own.[60] In fact, he goes so far as to say he follows his authority word-for-word (*e. g., Tales,* VIII, 78–84). It is the poet's duty to follow his source verbatim — the poet has no freedom at all, as Chaucer says in the prologue to the *Tales:*

But first I pray yow, of youre curteisye,
That ye n'arette it nat my vileynye,
Thogh that I pleynly speke in this mateere,
To telle yow hir wordes and hir cheere,
Ne thogh I speke hir wordes proprely.
For this ye knowen al so wel as I,
Whoso shal telle a tale after a man,
He moot reherce as ny as evere he kan
Everich a word, if it be in his charge,
Al speke he never so rudeliche and large,
Or ellis he moot telle his tale untrewe,
Or feyne thyng, or fynde wordes newe.
He may nat spare, althogh he were his brother;

(I, 725–37)

Thus he says the poet has no authority or responsibility even for *language*. He talks of "englishing" the "naked text." His statement near the end of *Troilus and Criseyde* that he would rather not blame Criseyde and that the real moral of the poem is that women should beware treachery, and his statement at the end of *The Clerk's Tale* that women should not put up with abuse — these too become part of his general campaign to deny his freedom and responsibility for the words he has put on paper.

But when Chaucer protests too much, the reader learns to look twice. Here too Chaucer does a very strange dance: he cites authors when he is not following them; he cites authors whom he never follows; he apparently even invents authors that never existed. One of the most interesting cases occurs in *The Hous of Fame,* when he says he is not following any author at all and then goes on to cite Vergil and Ovid (1. 314). Strangest of all, he *never anywhere* cites the author from whom he borrows most, Boccaccio. He borrows the "straight man" or "straw man" passages from Boethius and leaves out Dame Philosophy's clear statements of the truth to which they were building. Clearly he takes pleasure in being oblique in this matter of authors and authority.

All this irony could be said simply to reverse the denials: we conclude Chaucer *is* free to use his sources as he wishes. Yet we know more than a little about Chaucer and his sources: how much he borrowed; how closely he followed; how much genuine reverence he had for what is an "old book." Chaucer is not using simple irony here to make the *single* assertion that he is absolutely free. He is using complex irony and asserting both sides. The question "Which of you wrote this poetry" — like the question "Which of you spouses is in charge here" — leads inevitably to the wrong answer. Thus Chaucer implies a paradoxical and at times transcendent relationship of *participation* between the poet and his sources, just as he does between husband and wife in the paradigmatic marriage. "Where is authorship?" and "Where is 'maistrie'?" yield the same answer — simultaneously in neither and both.

This model gives the best reading for the passage at the end of *Troilus and Criseyde* wherein Chaucer tells his little tragedy not to envy the works of Vergil, Ovid, Homer, Lucan, and Statius. As a protestation of extreme modesty it is fitting and accurate for this mostly borrowed poem. Were it not a great work, it would be merely a translation of Boccaccio with verbatim digressions from Boethius. But on the other hand, Chaucer is doing what he saw Dante do in his *Inferno* IV, however much he avoids Dante's blatant arrogance: he is setting his name as author of this work among the names of the greatest writers known.[61] And this too, as Chaucer must have known perfectly well, was also wholly fitting.

A small detail illustrates Chaucer's habit of showing the coexistence of freedom and necessity. At the beginning of the pilgrimage the pilgrims draw straws in order to make random (one kind of freedom) the choice of who should begin the storytelling:

> ... [s]hortly for to tellen as it was,
> Were it by aventure, or sort, or cas,
> The sothe is this, the cut fil to the Knyght,
> Of which ful blithe and glad was every wyght,
> And telle he moste his tale, as was resoun,
> By foreward and by composicioun.
>
> (I, 843–48)

The redundancy — "were it by aventure, or sort, or cas" — is a signal to look twice. The man most highborn, most benign and humane, who ought to lead the others, who is in fact described before the others in the prologue, and whose selection makes everyone most happy, turns out to draw the straw: "And telle he moste his tale, as was resoun." The "resoun" seems quietly to refer not only to their agreement of the night before but also to a "resoun" in the nature of things by which this free random event led to exactly the arrangement that any benign God or orderly society would call for.

Chaucer treats the problem of freedom and necessity in various transformations, but always as an opposition or conflict that is transcended. A few exemplary images stay in mind: Troilus looking down from the eighth sphere upon "this litel spot of erthe that with the se embraced is"; the lonely combat between Palamon and Arcite in the woods, the crowded tournament in the elaborate arena, and the solemn funeral, all occurring on the same spot of ground; and proud Chauntecleer strutting in his tiny chicken yard. Each is an image of the world as a narrow "foule prisoun." Yet Chaucer affirms full freedom and responsibility in this seemingly cramped human situation.

VI. IRONY RELINQUISHED

AFTER I had learned the many ways in which Chaucer sets up oppositions and then affirms them equally, I came to realize — reluctantly at first — that in the endings of his two major works, *Troilus and Criseyde* and *The Canterbury Tales,* he does exactly the opposite. In each case there is an opposition, but instead of transcending it, Chaucer comes down squarely on one side, saying that it is right and that the other is wrong.

Although *Troilus and Criseyde* as a whole pulls us insistently in two directions at once with its detached and involved views of events, and although the ending confirms our participation in both the view from heaven and the view from earth, nevertheless Chaucer unequivocally says in the end that the view from heaven is right and the view from "this wrecched world," where all is "vanite," is wrong.

And such is the case with *The Canterbury Tales* too. It opens with a genial resolution of a whole set of oppositions: secular/religious; physical/spiritual; sexual/holy. The famous opening lines resolve the widest spectrum of events into one profound springing of transcendent life-giving juice: God's flowing grace; the martyr's flowing blood; the human impulse to make a pilgrimage; the desire to get out of doors and meet new people after winter; the pricking in the hearts of birds that sing all night; the blowing of the spring breeze; the spring rain's piercing to the root. Yet the whole poem ends by denying this synthesis. *The Parson's Tale* clearly ends the poem, and in the closing retraction the poet denies and disowns his writing and even professes to have forgotten anything wordly he has written.

In these two endings Chaucer relinquishes sophistication, complex irony, and dialectic when he has them most at his command. In doing so, he adds a completing element to his poetry. I can best explain how Chaucer does this by contrasting how Boethius and the Pardoner do not.

Compare how Chaucer and Boethius use their speaking voices. Chaucer begins both *Troilus* and the *Tales* with a richly ironic speaking voice — a persona: elusive, elaborately covered, paradoxical. In *Troilus* he talks of how he has no experience at all, and so forth and so forth; in the *Tales* he agrees solemnly with nearly every point of view represented by the pilgrims. But the endings of these two great poems are distinguished by the way Chaucer comes out from behind his persona with a voice that is loud, strong, and completely nonironic. *Troilus* ends with a veritable stretto of speakings in the poet's own voice. He speaks to his book, to us, to God, to young fresh folk, to Gower, and to translators. He insists here on the role of the poet as a man speaking directly to others, openly asking them to believe what he is trying to say.

Boethius, on the other hand, begins the *Consolation* speaking in his own voice and from a location in real time, but ends it in the abstract, disembodied voice of Dame Philosophy, not on earth, not in time. Boethius' own voice is ignored and forgotten.

Chaucer's final insistence on speaking in his own voice without irony amounts to a location of the poem in a real, historical personality and self — not in abstract language or truth. Individual tales too often end with a final bit of direct speech from the teller to the audience. In the retraction he refers specifically to himself as a poet and says that he cannot remember all the books he has written. He emphasizes his single location in real time:

from hennes forth unto my lyves ende...

and graunte me grace of verray penitence, confessioun and satisfacctioun to doon in this present lyf...

so that I may been oon of hem at the day of doom that shulle be saved.

He thereby avows that however successful his creation of a double point of view by manipulating words and concepts and by creating personae, nevertheless when it comes to living and acting, he has only one point of view and one point in time. And so though this religious affirmation is a choosing of what is heavenly and in this sense "upper," the *act of choosing* is the important action here, and it is essentially a coming downwards to accept his limited, single, human position on earth. Chaucer avows, in short, that it is necessary to come down from above, to inhabit this single point of view, and to make choices between oppositions — even though it would be more comfortable to float above and enjoy irony, multiple points of view, and the knowledge that hard choices can always be evaded by transcending them.

Chaucer's endings, then, in spite of the Boethian echoes, do not achieve relief from the single human point of view as the ending of the *Consolation* does; they do not achieve Boethius' lofty detached freedom. Chaucer may evoke the Boethian images of "casting the eyes upwards" and "returning home," but the ending does not give the reader a sense of soaring upwards to freedom. In Orpheus' death, Boethius moves the reader from genuine grief, associated with going down into the earth, to a soaring out above grief, above the earth. Even though Troilus too moves up to the eighth sphere when he dies, Chaucer makes the mood of the ending one of sad submission more than one of relieved unfettering. (The Middle English "sad" means "heavy.") When Chaucer calls his book a "tragedeye," he is calling it a story that ends in a downward direction. The ending and all the objects of the "lo here" and "swich fyn" stanzas are bathed in loss and sadness.

There is the same downward pointing to human limitation and singleness at the end of *The Canterbury Tales* in the down-to-earth Parson's humble tale and Chaucer's penitent retraction. Where Dame Philosophy stresses freedom, Chaucer's retraction describes his whole life's writing in terms of helplessness:

. . . if ther be any thyng in it that liketh hem, that thereof they thanken oure Lord Jhesu Christ, of whom procedeth al wit and al goodnesse. And if ther be any thyng that displese hem, I preye hem also that they arrette it to the defaute of myn unkonnynge, and nat to my wyl, that wolde ful fayn have seyd bettre if I hadde had konnynge.

Chaucer's *Book of the Duchess* is a consolation that we can compare with Boethius' *Consolation*. Boethius consoles by granting perspective, distance, and freedom from overwhelming grief. Chaucer consoles in the opposite fashion, by immersion in grief. Chaucer's poem offers a harrowing catharsis in which the very experience of grief and helplessness is recreated for John of Gaunt and the reader. Where Boethius offers escape from a limited and single point of view, Chaucer insists on inhabiting it fully.

The Pardoner, perhaps the most intriguing and haunting character in Chaucer, is strikingly like his creator except that the Pardoner does not relinquish irony. He is better with words than any of the other characters, a better poet and storyteller, more ironical and paradoxical. Chaucer gives the Pardoner a vocation very like his own. Poetry and preaching were simply two branches of medieval rhetoric, the art of trying to affect an audience with words. In addition, both the Pardoner and Chaucer give the same ironic twist to rhetoric. They turn out words that most listeners enjoy and benefit from without understanding them in the complex way the speaker does. Often, in fact, the audience and the speaker have opposite understand-ings. The Pardoner's normal preaching impels the hearers toward heaven and the speaker toward hell. He clearly loves giving these radically opposed valences to words.

Both Chaucer and the Pardoner enjoy watching themselves. Chaucer relishes the coy little portraits of the "Chaucers" scattered through his poetry. The Pardoner too likes to stand outside himself and see the irony and double meanings in his words and actions:

> Thus kan I preche agayn that same vice
> Which that I use, and that is avarice.
> But though myself be gilty in that synne,
> Yet kan I maken oother folk to twynne
> From avarice, and soore to repente.
>
> (VI, 427–31)

While the Friar and the Summoner also give clear, damning portraits of themselves — the Friar of his own robust combativeness and the Summoner of his own nastier vindictiveness — they do not realize they are describing themselves; they think they are describing and satirizing each other. The Pardoner, on the other hand, sets out to give a damning portrait of himself, does it well, and takes pleasure in it.

The Pardoner is ostensibly — and in a sense actually — completely frank with the pilgrims. He drops his mask and tells the truth. But though the words are literally true, they are still ironic: the Pardoner *means* something tricky and double-edged. Operationally, a reader never sees him face-to-face, never hears his real voice. Chaucer's "confessions" that he has never had any experience of life or love except from dreams, poems, or books are comparable but cruder examples of *apparent* candor. But whereas Chaucer in the endings of his poems actually does drop his mask and speak in his real voice, the Pardoner concludes with an intensification of his paradoxical hiddenness: his response to the anger of the host is silence and, finally, a kiss.

This view of the Pardoner clarifies the incident at the end of his sermon when he asks the pilgrims to come up and kiss his fake relics and give him money. It is hard to explain why this ending feels peculiarly right. Why should he ask them to do what will obviously infuriate them? The answer is that he is a compulsive ironist. His normal preaching is holiness to listeners, blasphemy to self. With the pilgrims he moves to a new level. He reveals the fraudulence of his words and *still* makes his words perform their old magic. His power over words, like a poet's, gives him power over the thoughts and feelings of his audience, and he can move the listeners toward heaven in spite of their knowledge that the words are fraudulent. He forcibly conjures up inside his audience a redemptive awareness of death and a revulsion at greed and violence. The exhilaration of doing this impels him — even though part of him must know he cannot succeed — into trying to climax his ironic dance by producing not just thoughts and feelings but behavior as well.

There is a compulsive shape to this whole sequence. He must know, really, what the outcome will be, but he allows himself either to blink his eyes somehow or to give in anyway. And then he experiences the thud of recognition in silence — the silence that comes from trying to digest what he has brought down upon himself. And with it comes a renewed sense of his detachment from all other humans.

Irony and dialectic are undertakings that yield detachment and, above all, control. Boethius' *Consolation* moves from loss of control toward perfect control. In the character of the Pardoner too perfect control is central. He never loses his control over himself, except perhaps that he cannot seem to stop himself from trying to increase his control over others, as when he tries to manipulate the pilgrims into kissing his relics. In the face of the host's strong abuse at the end, the Pardoner's self-control clamps down even tighter.

With respect to language there is a direct link between irony and control. Irony could be described as a speaker's way of trying to maintain control over his meaning. When Chaucer or the Pardoner uses irony, neither can be clearly pinned down as to his meaning; each always seems to be able to wriggle out of any interpretation put on his words. When Chaucer relinquishes irony, however, he hands his meaning more directly to his audience and consequently relinquishes a measure of control. People who love control often love irony.[62]

Throughout his poetry, Chaucer characteristically keeps this delicate ironic control. He is always playing tricks on us by making us notice — through a kind of time bomb his words plant in our heads — that our naive reading of some passage shows us to be foolish or morally obtuse. Initially, we accept the portrait of the Prioress, for example; we are charmed, we admire her. And then something makes us do a double-take: we realize that not only have we been shown a picture of moral obtuseness, but the very fact that we missed it makes us obtuse in the same way. (Only a few readers are sophisticated and ironic enough — guarded enough — never to be taken in even on a first reading.) This constant tricking, this constant retention to himself of his meaning, might seem intolerable — and many readers have exactly that response — but for the redeeming nonirony when Chaucer relinquishes control. At the end of *Troilus* and the *Tales,* particularly, there is a strong sense of submission, giving in, letting go, which is just what the Pardoner is incapable of.

This comparison of Chaucer and the Pardoner makes more concrete what is often only a cerebral-sounding paradox: that submission can yield a kind of freedom. It might seem that the Pardoner is especially free in being able to see exactly what he is doing and to do it anyway. He is faintly analogous, in this respect to Chauntecleer. But in fact there is a kind of claustrophobia in the way the Pardoner seems trapped behind his mask and his spectator's view of himself.

Thus it is not really true that the Pardoner is guilty of the very sin he understands so well, preaches against, and frees others from, namely, greed. Perhaps he has some greed, but it really serves to cover up the more complex sin of *mere sophistication* — sophistication never relinquished. We see no compulsive appetite for money or goods in either his words or his actions. But we do see a compulsive appetite for complexity. Thus Chaucer gives us a man capable of achieving great irony and sophistication — one who has the ability to see things from more than one point of view and thus to consider himself from, as it were, a God's-eye view as well as a human view — but incapable of the redeeming ability to shed this irony and become fully human. He is unable to waive paradox, and descend into full interpretation of his self.

This interpretation explains the reader's relief at the host's final gross response to the Pardoner. We need something strong to dispel this fear that comes from being so close to a man paralyzed as a spectator of himself. At some primal level he cannot activate himself. To change the terminology, Chaucer is dealing with the mystery of grace, the mystery of the sin against the Holy Spirit. The Pardoner plays God. To damn himself — which is what the Pardoner does — is the closest man can come to being God. And once he gets very far down that path, he is helpless to stop. If no grace is forthcoming, we feel at least some relief in gross physicality. The body seems to be an antidote both for irony and for paralysis.

These complex character traits suggest another important figure. Pandarus too is, like Chaucer, a master of words, a master of control and manipulation. He always sees things with an ironic perspective that leads him to chuckle. But despite his chuckle, his perspective and detachment give him a fatalistic sense that he himself cannot be happy. He has a spectator's position in life — as Chaucer professes to have — and he does much of his living vicariously. He acts for others, not for himself. But Chaucer shows, through Troilus' flight to the eighth sphere, that Pandarus' perspective is not a true or complete one. In Pandarus, as in the Pardoner, there is a sense of incomplete self-habitation. Pandarus sees ironically and uses multiple points of view rather than take the chance of immersion into the self's necessarily single point of time and perception.

But in Pandarus' final comment that he hates Criseyde and always will, there is a sense that he too is relinquishing irony. The occasion is again an ending. His words are a kind of "retraction" by the man who was the "poet" — the maker or manipulator — of *Troilus and Criseyde*:

> "What sholde I seyen? I hate, ywys, Cryseyde;
> And, God woot, I wol hate hire evermore!"
>
> .   .   .   .   .   .
>
> "If I dide aught that myghte liken the,
> It is me lief; and of this tresoun now,
> God woot that it a sorwe is unto me!
> And dredeles, for hertes ese of yow,
> Right fayn I wolde amende it, wiste I how.
> And fro this world, almyghty God I preye
> Delivere hire soon! I kan namore seye."
>
> (V, 1732–43)

In fact his words are reminiscent of Chaucer's retraction — or Chaucer's retraction echos Pandarus' — and there is the same somewhat prayerlike sense of submitting, giving in, and releasing control.

The intriguing similarities between Chaucer and

these two characters, and Chaucer's relinquishing of irony in his two major endings, suggest that Chaucer might have come to feel the danger that irony can pose to full participation in life. His little portraits of himself as narrator are always portraits of a person not fully alive, a person who gets experience only in surrogate ways, in books or dreams or writing. I cannot help guessing that the joke, like so many in Chaucer, is not just a joke.

The value of dialectic and complex irony is that they give relief from the limitations of normal language and thought and the single human point of view, relief from so many of the constrictions of life: having to make a limiting choice when both alternatives are right and desirable, having to commit oneself when the consequences are unknown, having to take full responsibility for one's words when the implications are not clear, and most of all having to relinquish some control. But what Chaucer ultimately reveals is that one cannot entirely remove the trapped or prisonlike quality of human life — or at least one cannot do so without losing some of one's humanity.

I believe nonirony in Chaucer's poetry to be a positive attainment. In his earlier poems the irony is heavy and unrelenting. The later moments in which Chaucer relinquishes irony manage to pervade our sense of the whole of his poetry, and thereby keep his persistent irony and double vision from being ultimately inhuman.

VII. THE VALUE OF DIALECTIC

CHAUCER was interested in the problem of freedom and necessity, and he often wrote about it even when he seemed to be writing about something else. In writing about Chaucer, I find that I have also been exploring the nature of knowledge and understanding. I cannot resist speculating here about why Chaucer's handling of oppositions seems so important. In doing so I plunge in over my head. In previous chapters I have tried to *demonstrate* my contentions; here I can only try to assert them plausibly.

If I were writing about the dative ending in Chaucer, I should perhaps see his dative endings as the source of his greatness. I temper the claim here only slightly. I do not think his dialectic is what makes him a great poet, but I do think that it makes him a wise one.

In trying to understand *Troilus and Criseyde* fully, I found a pattern of thinking at the center of the work. As I explored this pattern in more and more works by Chaucer, I came to see it as a source of the poet's wisdom. And in the process I began to see this pattern more and more often outside Chaucer in cases of great insight or intellectual progress. What I want to illustrate in this conclusion is that wisdom often seems to have this characteristic, dialectical shape.

The ancient sense of the word dialectic refers to the use of conflict — originally just of dialogue — in the search for truth. Hegel gave the narrower sense that is now current: the thesis-antithesis-synthesis pattern wherein two contradictory elements are transcended, and the process leads to a new idea on a higher level. Chaucer's dialectic falls between the ancient and the modern senses. He seldom produces the new idea on a higher level, though he does not just give a simple conflict either. By setting up a polar opposition and affirming both sides, he lays the groundwork for a broader frame of reference, ensuring that neither side can "win." He arranges the dilemma so that we can only be satisfied by taking a larger view. Sometimes he even creates that larger view.

Why should this pattern of thought make someone wiser, help to free someone from the limitations of language, logic, and the single human point of view? The answer has to do with the nature of knowing, with the way humans perceive and categorize. Perceiving is not so much like a camera's taking into itself an image of what is outside; it is more nearly like constructing or sculpting or drawing something from fragments of a view — or fragments of many views, in fact, as the eyes refuse to remain still. Even though the eye's lens projects an image onto the retina, the mind or brain cannot "take in" that image. It can only take in electrical impulses that are nothing like an image, and it must construct from these impulses our sense of what we see. In short, "seeing, hearing, and remembering are all acts of construction which may make more or less use of stimulus information depending on circumstances."[63] That perception is active and constructive is vividly dramatized by hallucinations: there is no way to distinguish between hallucinating and perceiving as processes. Both result from taking limited, fragmentary stimulus information and constructing a picture or idea. The only difference is that we do a better job when we succeed in having an accurate perception.[64]

A comparable process occurs at a higher level in categorizing and thinking. We do not just *get* concepts and ideas, we *make* them — even when we seem like passive receivers of information. Hence our already existing categories or frames of reference necessarily shape any new category since they are the only source of rules for how to make up a new one.[65] Thus new material is often distorted or ignored when it is "cognitively dissonant" in relation to the existing structures.

Contemporary psychologists thus confirm the cognitive relativity formulated by Boethius: knowledge is always a product of the knower as much as of the thing known. To be more exact, knowledge is a result of the interaction between the knower and the object of knowledge. If there are no contrasting channels for verifying our knowledge — if, for example, we cannot touch or otherwise learn about the things that we try to see — then there is no way to know how much or what sort of distortion has crept in.

This epistemological dilemma shows up most vividly in the realm where knowers have pushed furthest and tried for the most objectivity: particle physics. Physicists cannot get information about a particle alone. They can only get a package of information about the interaction of the particle and the "observer" (*i. e.,* the equipment). They can know the velocity of a particle, but not its location, or its location but not its velocity; but they can never know both.

In social science too there is a growing recognition of how the "observer" affects the results of an experiment through the mechanics of the experimental situation and the preconceptions of the designer. In the case of subjective knowledge, the act of focusing our attention on a thought or feeling inevitably alters it.

The dialectical pattern of thinking provides some relief from this structural difficulty inherent in knowing. Since perception and cognition are processes in which the organism "constructs" what it sees or thinks according to models already there, the organism tends to throw away or distort material that does not fit this model. The surest way to get hold of what your present frame blinds you to is to try to adopt the opposite frame, *i. e.,* to reverse your model. A person who can live with contradiction and exploit it — who can use conflicting models — can simply see and think *more.*[66] If I think of my behavior as free, the best way to notice and understand behavior that was hidden from me is to try to see it as determined.

If in particular we are trying to know something that is especially hard to check or verify, our best hope of doing so is to gain as many *different* and *conflicting* knowings as possible. Holding all these conflicting views in mind, we must then try to get a sense of the unknown behind them. People who are good at doing this seem to call upon some subtle tact, judgment, or intuition. I think that they are using a metaphorical, analogical, *Gestalt*-finding kind of ability.[67] They are good at maintaining contradictory points of view simultaneously and at living with ambiguity in order to refrain from premature resolution. They can wait for contrary knowings to interact and affect each other so that the metaphors, analogues, or *Gestalten* that eventually emerge are likelier to reflect more fully the unknown new phenomena and less likely merely to replicate the patterns already present in the mind.[68]

Searching for contradiction and affirming both sides can allow you to find both the limitations of the system in which you are working and a way to break out of it. If you find contradictions and try too quickly to get rid of them, you are only neatening up, even strengthening, the system you are in. To actually get beyond that system you need to find the deepest contradictions and, instead of trying to reconcile them, heighten them by affirming both sides. And if you can nurture the contradictions cleverly enough, you can be led to a new system with a wider frame of reference, one that includes the two elements which were felt as contradictory in the old frame of reference.

When Einstein found contradictions in classical Newtonian mechanics — contradictions concerning the speed of light in the Michelson-Morley experiment that others tried to eliminate — he developed a theory of relativity that saved the contradictory results. He did not really vanquish Newtonian mechanics, but he radically limited its application. What looked like a general universal law (classical mechanics) was shown to be really just a special, limited case within a more general law of wider application (the general theory of relativity). What looks like polar opposition is really a case of one being a subset of the other — just as Boethius sees the cave/sky opposition as really a matter of the cave being a subset of the sky.

Analogously, Chaucer uses contradiction in *The Knight's Tale* not only to uncover the limitations of the system in which he is working (chivalry), but also to suggest a new, larger system (the values Theseus embodies). Chaucer pushes the opposition between the two cousins till it reaches contradiction — till the rules of the original system lead to a dead end or a wrong conclusion — and thereby forces into the open the weaknesses or limitations of the system of chivalric romance. Courage, loyalty, and honor are shown to comprise a special, limited system of values that is only a subset of Theseus' larger system, which contains feeling for others, humor, irony, forgiveness, the ability to change one's mind, and the ability to grow and change through suffering instead of just stoically enduring it. If courage, loyalty, and honor are applied too widely, they lead to brutal, rigid, humorless, and even unfeeling behavior, and hence contradict the larger system. But if, as a special case, they are limited to their proper sphere of application, they are fine and there is no conflict.

However, Chaucer usually just breaks out of the limited system he is in by finding and affirming contradictions in it, without going on to present a new, larger system. For example, his preoccupation with the conflict between freedom and necessity often takes the form of asking, in effect, "Which of you is in charge here?" — of husband and wife, poet and sources, man and God — and then watching contradictions emerge. Was it Criseyde, Troilus, Pandarus, the war, or Fate which separated Troilus and Criseyde? Again, no single answer is satisfactory. The truth is contradictory. Chaucer, by exploiting contradiction, is uncovering the limits or blind spots in the system for understanding freedom and responsibility when more than one person is involved.

He does not provide a new system, but he suggests, at least, that two or more people together can seem to function like a complex organism or system. When this system functions as it ought, *each* party seems to have complete freedom and authority: things occur just as planned by *both* man and God, husband and wife, poet and sources. But when the system is not working, somehow things do not come out as either planned. Between them, their freedom and authority do not even seem to add up to 100%. The system rides them. With freedom and responsibility, of course, goes fault. Chaucer implies that fault proliferates along with control: the wife's mistake is the fault of the husband and vice versa (*The Franklin's Tale, The Mer-*

*chant's Tale); the poet's mistake is the fault of the sources and vice versa ("Do not blame me, dear reader . . ."); and even man's mistake is a "fault" which Christ takes on through participation (in the basic meaning of the crucifixion; compare, by analogy, "patient" Griselda). Husband and wife, poet and sources, man and God are all implied somehow to inhere each in the other in a relationship of participation.

Much work in our own century confirms Chaucer's implication that we need some larger system or systems for trying to talk about individual agency and functioning when more than one individual is involved. A number of quite diverse people are now engaged in trying to develop such systems by different methods — systems analysis, cybernetics, group-process psychology, R. D. Laing's school of psychiatry (which treats the family as a single organism), and ecology (which treats the individual or the whole population as only part of a system that includes neighbors and environment). After a new system is comfortably worked out, the conventional way of dividing freedom and control — as if each individual were free and entirely self-contained — will probably remain as a special case that gives valid answers and does not cause contradiction when applied within its appropriate limits.

Exploiting contradiction helps bring to light the unnoticed limitations of that system we work in most closely, the one whose blind spots are hardest to notice: language. Efforts to uncover the limitations of language and logic seem to be the hallmark of the twentieth century. When physicists conceive of light as both wave and particle, they are putting into our hardest currency the idea that the "real thing" is un-renderable with our standard linguistic-logical equip-ment, and that we render it best by forcibly bending contradictory models into intersection. General rela-tivity is a rebuke to our linguistically ingrained con-ceptions space, time, mass, and velocity. Benjamin Whorf asserts the relativity of perception because of the relativity of linguistic structure. Existentialists and phenomenologists emphasize how language falsi-fies actual experience. In the Middle Ages there was a greater sense of the limitations of language than in any other period but our own, and I think this is a major reason for the increased modern interest in that pe-riod.

The Nun's Priest's Tale is a late, sophisticated work in which Chaucer deals almost directly with the limitations of language. Using a mock-heroic in which animals think and speak, Chaucer writes in effect about the tricky, paradoxical relationship between ut-terance and behavior — between mind and body, man and animal. It is a poem about the marvel and ab-surdity of a physical body that speaks and thinks.

By exploiting the contradictions that occur at the intersection of behavior and utterance — the contra-dictions between, as it were, Chauntecleer's smart mind and stupid body (or his smart body and stupid mind) — Chaucer forces out into the open the limitations of the categories for talking about both behavior and utterance. In the confusion, he enriches each by the other. On the one hand, he shows that utterance is often best understood as behavior. All of Chauntecleer's learned talk is not really so much about what it professes to be about — he seems to ignore or forget what he has argued for — but rather serves as behavior expressing his sense of self-importance in the universe and his lordship over his wife. His learned footnotes are momentary preenings of his tail feathers. On the other hand, Chaucer also shows that behavior is often best understood as utterance: Chauntecleer and Pertelote speak more clearly in behavior than in words.

Chaucer is showing the need for a satisfactory larger system for speaking clearly about behavior and utterance and their interrelation. That is precisely what many significant twentieth-century thinkers are working on. For example, J. L. Austin, in his general theory of speech acts, rethinks speech as a subset of the larger category of behavior. He chides philosophers for always thinking of utterance in terms of true and false:

What we have to study is *not* the sentence but the issuing of an utterance in a speech situation. . . . It is essential to realize that "true" and "false", like "free" and "unfree", do not stand for anything simple at all; but only for a general dimension of being a right or proper thing to say as opposed to a wrong thing, in these circumstances, to this audience, for these purposes and with these intentions. . . . The truth and falsity of a statement depend not merely on the meanings of words but on what act you were performing in what circumstance.[69]

Speech, as just a special case of behavior, is subject to the "ills that all action is heir to . . . subject to the usual troubles and reservations about attempt as distinct from achievement, being intentional as distinct from being unintentional, and the like."[70] Austin makes the question of whether statements are true or false into a special, limited case or subset of the whole larger system for understanding the "force" or "effects" of action:

> [Stating and describing] have no unique position over the matter of being related to facts in a unique way called being true or false, because truth and falsity are . . . not names for relations, qualities, or what not, but for a dimension of assessment — how the words stand in respect of satisfactoriness to the facts, events, situations, &c., to which they refer.[71]

Freud too brings behavior and utterance together into one system. Where Austin treats utterance as behavior, Freud treats behavior as utterance. Ostensibly he uses a system modeled on classical mechanics with the emphasis on cause. But in fact he keeps coming up with what Chaucer implied: "overdetermined behavior" — events with too many causes. We see why he does this when we see *what* behavior he is drawn to look at: language or utterance — dreams and slips of the tongue. Freud's gift may be that he taught us to ask, when we wish to understand a piece of behavior, not "What caused him to do that?" but rather "What does it mean? What is he saying?" And the weaknesses in psychoanalytical practice may come from the extent to which it still clings to a physical, etiological model:

What Freud did here was not to explain the patient's choice causally but to understand it and give it meaning, and the procedure he engaged in was not the scientific one of elucidating causes but the semantic one of making sense of it. It can indeed be argued that much of Freud's work was really semantic and that he made a revolutionary discovery in semantics, viz. that neurotic symptoms are meaningful disguised communications, but that, owing to his scientific training and allegiance, he formulated his findings in the conceptual framework of the physical sciences. In some aspects of his work Freud saw this himself clearly. His most famous work he entitled *The Interpretation of Dreams* not *The Cause of Dreams* and his chapter on symptoms in his *Introductory Lectures* is called *The Sense of Symptoms*. He was also well aware that many of his ideas had been anticipated by writers and poets rather than by scientists.[72]

To shift explanation from cause to meaning is to shift some of the focus from the past to the future. There is necessarily a teleological aspect to speech, an attempt to make something happen in the future.

There may be a clue here to the larger system that will eventually emerge to permit us to speak more clearly about the relationship between behavior and utterance. Utterance may be the most useful paradigm for behavior. At this point, at least, from our knowledge of how language and poetry work, we understand better how there may be two or more contradictory meanings in a set of words than we understand how there may be two or more contradictory causes for an event.[73]

Karl Popper, in an article called "What is Dialectic?" argues in a no-nonsense tone that the power of contradiction lies merely in its repugnance:

It cannot be emphasized too strongly that if we change this attitude, and decide to put up with contradictions, then contradictions must at once lose any kind of fertility. They would no longer be productive of intellectual progress. For if we were prepared to put up with contradictions, pointing out contradictions in our theories could no longer induce us to change them. In other words, all criticism (which consists in pointing out contradictions) would lose its force. Criticism would be answered by "And why not?" or perhaps even by an enthusiastic "There you are!"; that is, by welcoming the contradictions which have been pointed out to us.[74]

Surely he is right to criticize extreme dialecticians who seek an end to traditional logic altogether. But though contradiction is an itch we naturally seek to remove, Popper seems in such a *hurry* to remove it. A major part of his essay is devoted to showing rigorously that contradiction is meaningless and useless because in logic, two contradictory statements entail *any* statement. But though this may be true in strict logic, when it comes to the actual process of getting ideas, seeing where they lead, and even assessing their worth, a particular contradiction can be meaningful indeed, and can point in a very particular direction. Furthermore, contradictions *cannot* always be removed quickly. For a long time physics has put up with the definition of light as both wave and particle. Some physicists say this contradiction is permanent.[75] And Thomas Kuhn's account of the history of science[76] implies that the actual process of deciding between competing models is not one that can be performed by strict logic but rather one in which authorities in the field are implicitly empowered to decide the question on grounds — pragmatic, aesthetic, analogical — that are difficult to specify.[77]

Popper insists that dialectic is a "descriptive" theory not a "fundamental" one: descriptive in that it describes stages that actual ideas or theories sometimes go through in their development, but not fundamental, not a "theory of all sorts of inferences [like logic] used all the time by all sciences."[78] He talks as if this were a logical matter, but it is really an empirical question: how often *are* various patterns of thinking actually used? We need to find out. In making this distinction he is trying, in effect, to keep the time dimension out of thinking. He is willing, that is, to accept a temporal or historical account of the stages through which the opinions of some person or group passed, but he does not want a temporal account of the actual thinking process itself. He insists that valid inference occurs only in the realm of an abstract, timeless logic.

Perhaps he is right. I am no philosopher or logician. But everything I am discussing in this chapter makes me feel that there is something particularly important about bringing time into a realm where it has been absent. What was perhaps Hegel's central act was to introduce the time dimension into the hitherto timeless realm of "pure" thinking and inference by insisting that you cannot talk about what is true or what follows from something without talking about *when*. And Hegelians insist that time is the *source* of contradiction, that it is in the realm of time that things or ideas move toward their opposites. Though I cannot evaluate the logic or ontology of these kinds of assertions, many important systematic breakthroughs in thinking seem to involve just this pattern of bringing time into a realm where it has been absent.

For example, the three giant theories of the nineteenth century — those of Darwin, Marx, and Freud — are all cases of insisting on an historical or developmental model. Darwin found the key to understanding the *form* of an organism by seeing where it stands in an historical developmental process. Marx did the same thing to explain a social structure; Freud to explain human behavior. At one point in the developmental or historical process, a phenomenon might mean one thing; at another it might mean something entirely different. Without the time dimension, the explanation is meaningless. Einstein's theory of relativity is, of course, the most striking instance of a theory that insists on the time dimension (the "fourth" dimension) to make sense of phenomena in which it had not seemed to be needed before. Piaget, who considers himself a philosopher and logician as much as an empirical psychologist, has given a powerful model for understanding thinking by also insisting on a developmental structure. And he argues that all growth results from the interaction in time of contradictory processes, assimilation and accommodation. His model has been fruitful in spawning others.[79]

Time needs to be brought into accounts of how language has meaning. Austin's theory of speech acts does so when he says you must consider all the surrounding circumstances in a speech act. I think Owen Barfield's work has power because he insists on the role of time in the meaning of words. For myself, it did not seem possible to give a satisfactory account of the meaning of the words of *Troilus and Criseyde* without talking about a temporal sequence of events within the reader — agreement, disagreement, and then agreement again.

Since Coleridge there has been a tradition of using the reconciliation of opposites as a model for imaginative art and of seeing metaphor as a microcosm of imaginative art.[80] My approach obviously grows out of this tradition. But the emphasis is usually on reconciling, bringing together, "fusing." Here I should like to give a bit more emphasis to the element of contradiction.

Monroe Beardsley is one of the few analysts of metaphor who bring to the fore what is the most important fact about metaphor: there must be a *contradiction*, a piece of *non*-sense, before you can have a metaphor.[81] The word or phrase must be sufficiently *wrong* to produce at least a momentary blockage of sense. This is illustrated by borderline cases: if you can feel *leg* as the wrong word in the phrase *the leg of the table* (*leg* perhaps as appropriate only to animate organisms), then you can feel *leg of the table* as a meta-phor. For most people the phrase is usually literal.

From the contradiction or *non*-sense comes the energy or force of a metaphor, the force that makes the mind jump the rails and do something different in the presence of the words from what it usually does. Metaphor has the dialectical pattern I have been exploring in Chaucer. The metaphor does not provide a new system or synthesis, it only provides an abutting of opposed elements. Thus metaphor can be described as a *refusal* to synthesize, a refusal to find new language, an insistence on letting the contradiction stand. When the metaphor is new and unusual, it forces the mind to do exactly what Chaucer forces us to do: simply to live with the contradiction and try to let it reverberate as a way of doing justice to the complexity of its subject.

It is useful to look at imaginative art as a whole in a similar light. Morse Peckham points out that although people talk more about the unity in art, the striking and useful thing is usually its lack of unity. He makes a psycho-biological argument: that the primary activity of the organism is to categorize — to see samenesses, although really everything is unique in some way. Otherwise prediction and survival are not possible. But categorizing falls into ruts and thereby often blinds one to what may be small but important differences. Art, Peckham argues usefully, is an activity that serves to break down habitual categories. It trains and rewards living with contradiction and disunity.[82]

I want to conclude by delimiting as clearly as possible what I am trying to assert. I am not saying that all these famous people actually used a dialectical pattern in their thinking (as I hope I showed Boethius and Chaucer did). I do not know the actual steps they followed in their thinking.[83] Nor am I espousing the philosophical position of Hegelianism with its ontology and determinism. I do maintain that many important insights or breakthroughs end up as a movement of thought from one frame of reference — originally taken as the whole frame of reference or the most universal way to conceive the matter — to a larger one. There appears to be a contradiction between the original and the new frame of reference — and/or between the original one and some consequence or branch of the new one. But the original one can finally be understood as a subset of the larger one, a special case that does not really contradict it if correctly restricted. If breakthroughs often have this shape, then the following are likely to be fruitful strategies: to search for potential contradictions in a given system; to heighten them by affirming both sides rather than trying to resolve or eliminate them immediately; to develop in general an attraction for contradiction, which I think Boethius and Chaucer had; and even to try negating or turning things upside down just to see what new comes to light. The goal is to encourage the growth of new and larger frames of reference out of the interaction of contradictions, but one should remember, nevertheless, not to be in too much of a hurry to get rid of the contradiction and find a new frame of reference. Taking enough time will increase the chances of doing justice to any possible novelty in the matter under investigation.

Certain people are especially smart. They have a talent for having good hunches, nurturing them, and having a sense of which ones to follow. In short, they are especially good at getting to the truth. These people are right too often for it to be a matter of luck. Nor could they have their success by simply cranking through blind algorithms. And they do not get there by strict logic — logic often comes only much later. If these people are not using strict logic, brute algorithm, or sheer luck, and they are still consistently insightful, there must be some patterns in their thinking, some lawfulness in their activity. Affirming contradictions and not being in too much of a hurry to get rid of them — Chaucer's dialectic — must be one of the patterns of thought that makes wise people wise.

NOTES

INTRODUCTION

1.   Quoted from Richard Green's translation, *The Consolation of Philosophy* (Indianapolis, 1962).

2.   See G. E. R. Lloyd, *Polarity and Analogy: Two Types of Argumentation in Early Greek Thought* (Cambridge University Press, 1966) for a detailed and interesting study of this matter. An introductory passage:

> Many factors appear to contribute to the remarkable prevalence of theories based on opposition in so many societies at different stages of technological development. First there is the fact that many prominent phenomena in nature exhibit a certain duality: day alternates with night; the sun rises in one quarter of the sky and sets in the opposite quarter; in most climates the contrast between the seasons (summer and winter, or dry season and rainy season) is marked; in the larger animals male and female are distinct, and the bilateral symmetry of their bodies is obvious. Secondly, the duality of nature often acquires an added significance as the symbolic manifestation of fundamental religious or spiritual categories: the classification of phenomena into opposite groups may reflect, and itself form an important part of, a system of religious beliefs which expresses the ideals of the society, and by which the whole life of the society is regulated. And then a third factor must also be taken into consideration: whether or not the terms are divided into a "positive" and a "negative" pole, opposites provide a simple framework of reference by means of which complex phenomena of all sorts may be described or classified. Antithesis is an element in

any classification, and the primary form of antithesis, one may say, is division into *two* groups — so that the *simplest* form of classification, by the same token, is a dualist one. (p. 80)

3. See C. S. Lewis, "Imagination and Thought in the Middle Ages," in *Studies in Medieval and Renaissance Literature* (Cambridge University Press, 1966):

> Faced with this self-contradictory corpus, they hardly ever decided that one of the authorities was simply right and the others wrong; never that all were wrong. To be sure, in the last resort it was taken for granted that the Christian writer must be right as against the pagans. But it was hardly ever allowed to come to the last resort. It was apparently difficult to believe that anything in the books . . . was just plumb wrong. No; if Seneca and St. Paul disagreed with one another, and both with Cicero, and all these with Boethius, there must be some explanation which would harmonize them. (p. 45)

4. "Chaucer the Pilgrim," PMLA, LXIX (1954), reprinted in T. Donaldson, *Speaking of Chaucer* (New York, 1970), p. 11.

5. Muscatine calls attention to Chaucer's "simultaneous awareness of different and opposite planes of reality," and his "double view of the same situation, producing where the two views are pointedly contrasted, a double irony" (*Chaucer and the French Tradition* [Berkeley, 1957], pp. 132, 153). Dorothy Everett speaks of "Chaucer's capacity for seeing his story and his characters from both inside and out, so that his readers can sympathize with the hero and at the same time see him and his doings in perspective" (*Essays on Middle English Literature* [Oxford, 1955], p. 85). Robert Payne talks of "that complex ironic perspective which has for so long seemed to modern readers distinctively Chaucerian," and says that one source of this perspective was "school rhetorics . . . raising questions about

the correlation of language with truth and volatile human emotion . . ." ("Chaucer and the Art of Rhetoric" in *Companion to Chaucer Studies,* ed. Beryl Rowland [Toronto, 1968], p. 55). Ida Gordon says that "the sympathy and fellow-feeling for the persons in the story which the narrative invites is itself essential to our full apprehension of the morality that the irony serves to define. . . . The narrative, for all its irony, [is] an encouragement to love, and enables us to see that, in the ultimate analysis, the poet is seeing his subject through, not with, an ironic eye" (*The Double Sorrow of Troilus: A Study of Ambiguities in Troilus and Criseyde* [Oxford, 1970], pp. 138, 142). For other pointings at my enterprise see C. S. Lewis, *The Allegory of Love* (London, 1936), p. 173; and Paul G. Ruggiers, *The Art of The Canterbury Tales* (Madison, 1965), pp. 156, 252–54.

6. D. W. Robertson, *A Preface to Chaucer* (Princeton, 1963), p. 51.

I. BOETHIUS' 'THE CONSOLATION OF PHILOSOPHY'

7. For a brief introduction to Boethius' life see Richard Green's introduction to the *Consolation,* pp. ix–xxiii. For fuller treatments see his selected bibliography, p. xxv; also Pierre Courcelle, *La Consolation de Philosophie dans la Tradition Littéraire* (Paris, 1967); and H. Liebeschuetz, "Western Christian Thought from Boethius to Anselm," in *Later Greek and Early Medieval Philosophy,* ed. A. H. Armstrong (Cambridge University Press, 1967), pp. 538–55, 587–93.

8. Pierre Courcelle, *Late Latin Writers and their Greek Sources,* trans. Harry E. Wedeck (Cambridge, Mass., 1969), p. 277. See also Courcelle, *La Consolation,* p. 215; and F. N. Robinson, ed., *The Works of Geoffrey Chaucer,* 2nd ed. (Boston, 1957), p. 319.

9. See Green's introduction to the *Consolation,* p. xiii,

and his references to the work of William Bark on this matter.

10. "Boethius never explained how he achieved the synthesis between his Neoplatonic philosophy and his Christian theology. . . . Thus, even for questions of faith Boethius confines himself to applying the rational method of the Platonic commentators on Aristotle, and the theology he expounds in the *De Consolatione Philosophiae* is in his view a purely rational theology" (Courcelle, *Late Latin Writers,* pp. 321–22). See also Courcelle, *La Consolation,* pp. 228–30, 340–42.

11. See Courcelle, *Late Latin Writers,* p. 318 for a brief review of the continuing debate on whether or not Boethius was really Christian. See also Courcelle, *La Consolation,* pp. 340 ff; and Liebeschuetz, p. 588.

12. Courcelle, *La Consolation,* pp. 175–76, 340–44.

13. See Courcelle, *Late Latin Writers,* p. 316: "Moreover, though a Christian, he does not hesitate to mention, even in his *Opuscula Theologica,* and to adopt on his own account, the doctrine of the perpetuity of the universe professed by the pagan Ammonius but passionately attacked by his Christian pupils Zacharias and Philoponus." Boethius makes the matter very clear:

> "Therefore they are wrong who . . . suppose that the created world is coeternal with its creator. For it is one thing to live an endless life, which is what Plato ascribed to the world, and another for the whole of unending life to be embraced all at once as present, which is clearly proper to the divine mind. . . . Therefore if we wish to call things by their proper names, we should follow Plato in saying that God indeed is eternal, but the world is perpetual." (v, Pr. 6)

14. Quotations from the *Consolation* are taken from Richard Green's translation and are followed in each case by the number of the book and section in parenthesis.

15. It is not quite true that *none* of the arguments for divine necessity contradict those for human freedom. There is a notably weak passage late in Book IV where Dame Philosophy speaks of God as a physician who does indeed meddle in human events to produce the outcomes He wants — meddles in such a fashion as clearly to undermine human freedom. For example, He doles out punishment to some because they can bear it, to others because it will correct them, and to yet others because it will be an example to the rest. A shot gun kind of argument. The passage is also weak in that it undermines the previous arguments for God's governance which insisted that wordly misfortune (such as Boethius' imprisonment) is not true misfortune: this passage treats such misfortune as genuine punishment planned by God.

16. In *Metaphor and Symbol,* ed. L. C. Knights and Basil Cottle (London, 1960), pp. 48–63.

17. The following passages consciously evoke the essential event in Plato's parable of the cave: the action of turning around and looking in the right direction and ceasing to look at mere shadows (an event, by the way, that gives Christianity its now buried metaphor of "conversion"):

> "Now turn your mind's eye in the opposite direction and there you will see the true happiness which I promised to show you." (III, Pr. 9)
> "When you have understood that, you may turn your attention in the opposite direction and then you will be able to recognize the nature of true blessedness." (III, Pr. 1)

See Book I, Pr. 7 for an explicit evocation of *The Dream of Scipio.* The sky image also evokes Plato's *Phaedrus.*

18. It is worth noting that Boethius also taps ancient connotations of heaven and hell, and archetypal connotations of male and female. Female: cave, dark, jewels, sweetness, loss of power, passivity, inferiority; male: power, light, up

in the air (erection), flying, cleanness, being calm and self-contained, not feeling need, superiority. See also Lloyd, *Polarity and Analogy:*

> Originally Yin is the "shady side" of a hill or house, Yang the "sunny side." On the one hand darkness, cold, the female sex, night, moon, earth, west, north, soft, heavy, weak, behind, below, right and death are Yin. On the other light (daylight), warmth, the male sex, day, sun, the heavens, east, south, hard, light (as opposed to heavy), strong, in front, above, left, and life are Yang. But this doctrine does not only apply to what we should term natural objects or phenomena: Yang is regarded as noble, Yin as common, so that on the one hand joy, wealth, honour, celebrity, love, profit and so on are considered as belonging to Yang, while on the other such things as sorrow, poverty, misery, bitterness, ignominy, rejection and loss belong to Yin. The notion of the interdependence of Yin and Yang was, moreover, a key doctrine of ancient Chinese speculative thought for many centuries. *I Ching*, or the *Book of Changes,* is a comprehensive pseudo-scientific system based on these opposites. (p. 35)

19.   The poetry in the *Consolation* is linked with music in that Boethius calls the poems *metra*. It is interesting that the most beautiful, even the most romantic and emotional, poetry of the *Consolation* occurs in Book III, which is also the most abstract and dialectical. It opens with Dame Philosophy saying Boethius must now prepare for "bitter medicine."

20.   The idea of four kinds of knowing seems to be Aristotelian. The Neoplatonists took it up and sometimes made it five. See Courcelle, *Late Latin Writers,* pp. 219–30.

21.   For an exploration of how metaphorical thinking works out implicitly what usually can only afterwards be brought to fruition through self-conscious logical thinking, see Peter Elbow, "Real Learning," *Journal of General Education,* July, 1971.

22. Boethius himself carved the very opposition that he here transcends:

> To provide an introduction to the study of logic he translated and commented on Porphyry's *Introduction to the Categories of Aristotle,* a book designed to introduce students to problems of dialectical and epistemological method; it was this commentary which provided the point of departure for the controversy between realists and nominalists on the existence of universals, which was to be so important in later Medieval philosophy. (Green, *Consolation,* p. xi)

See also H. R. Patch, *The Tradition of Boethius* (New York, 1935), p. 35; and Courcelle, *La Consolation,* pp. 220–21.

23. This hierarchical model for reconciling opposites by subordinating one to the other was no doubt partly a result of Boethius' working in the Neoplatonic tradition. Courcelle, speaking of Boethius' subordination of Fate to Providence, says, "This subordination, unknown to the Stoics, is meaningless except in a philosophy that establishes a hierarchy among beings, and it is among the Neoplatonists that we find the problem stated from this angle" (*Late Latin Writers,* p. 305).

II. 'TROILUS AND CRISEYDE'

24. An earlier version of this chapter was read at the English Institute Conference in 1966 and published in *Literary Criticism and Historical Understanding: English Institute Essays,* ed. Philip Damon (New York, 1967).

25. Quotations from Chaucer are from *The Works of Geoffrey Chaucer,* ed. F. N. Robinson, 2nd ed. (Boston, 1957).

26. See, for example, H. S. Bennet, *Chaucer and the Fifteenth Century* (London, 1947), p. 61; and W. Curry,

"Destiny in Troilus and Criseyde," in *Chaucer and the Medieval Sciences,* rev. ed. (London, 1960), p. 79.

27. In fact Troilus' long passage from Boethius is not in the alpha manuscript of *Troilus* "and seems to have been inserted by Chaucer after the main body of the narrative was composed" (Robinson, in his note to the speech, p. 830).

28. Curry, p. 29.

29. Bennet, p. 61, gives reasons for thinking that many in Chaucer's audience would have been familiar with Boethius' arguments. For others who have discussed the appropriateness of the speech to this context, see Robinson's note to it, p. 830.

30. Chauncy Wood, investigating Chaucer's use of astrology and astrological figures, shows how this and many other ascriptions to heavenly fortune seem more ironic than serious. See his *Chaucer and the Country of the Stars* (Princeton, 1970), especially pp. 44–50.

31. C. Muscatine, *Chaucer and the French Tradition* (Berkeley, 1957), p. 163.

32. Determinism does not necessarily inhere in this God's-eye foresight. Troilus thinks it does, and Chaucer allows the unphilosophical reader to think so too by omitting precisely those passages in Boethius where Dame Philosophy carefully shows that God's foreknowledge does *not* cause necessity.

33. Charles Owen, in *Chaucer Criticism,* ed. R. J. Schoeck and J. Taylor, 2 vols. (Notre Dame, 1961), II, explores these symmetries.

34. The extent of the comedy is sometimes underemphasized. Muscatine, pp. 153 ff., does it justice in a passage specifically exploring its effects.

35. See Donaldson's reading of the nearby stanza that

begins "O yonge, fresshe folkes" (v, 1835 ff.): "All the illusory loveliness of a world which is man's only reality is expressed in the very lines that reject that loveliness" ("The Ending of Chaucer's Troilus," in *Early English and Norse Studies,* ed. Arthur Brown and Peter Foote [London, 1963], reprinted in Donaldson's *Speaking of Chaucer* [New York, 1970], p. 98).

36.   See Donaldson later in the same essay (p. 100):

> Having painfully climbed close to the top of the ridge he did not want to climb, he cannot help looking back with longing at the darkening but still fair valley in which he lived; and every resolute thrust forward ends with a glance backward.
>
> In having his narrator behave thus, Chaucer has achieved a meaning only great poetry can achieve. The world he knows and the heaven he believes in grow ever farther and farther apart as the woeful contrast between them is developed, and ever closer and closer together as the narrator blindly unites them in the common bond of his love.

Ida Gordon, in her strong, well argued book *The Double Sorrow of Troilus,* stresses an implied reconciliation: how Boethian teaching and Christian doctrine — and in the light of them, the words of the poem — show that it *is* possible both to love sexually and to keep one's eye on God or one's own true home. Hers is a useful and important corrective in the long debate that tended to assume the absolute irreconcilability of the poem and its ending. I remain convinced, however, that the essential dynamic of the poem is one of pulling mercilessly in two directions at once, not of hinting at some higher, third way that will resolve the conflict. The resolution she points out, nevertheless, is precisely what the opposed pulling sets up the need for.

III. 'THE KNIGHT'S TALE'

37.   An earlier version of this chapter appeared in *Chaucer Review,* VII, No. 2 (1973).

38.   Whiting implies this same contrast of character when he says that "stronger characters in *The Knight's Tale,* Arcite and Theseus, use proverbs as the stronger characters do in Troilus and Criseyde." See B. J. Whiting, *Chaucer's Use of Proverbs* (Cambridge, Mass., 1934), p. 82.

39.   Robert A. Pratt writes shrewdly of this matter: "Palamon's complete submission to love and Venus perhaps makes him a little more attractive than the more practical and aggressive Arcite . . . [but] Chaucer wisely does not overdo the differentiation between these two." ("Chaucer's Use of the *Teseida*" in *Studies in Philology,* XLII, 745). Both Paul G. Ruggiers, *The Art of the Canterbury Tales* (Madison, 1965), p. 158, and Robert M. Jordan, *Chaucer and the Shape of Creation* (Cambridge, Mass., 1967), p. 173, cite this passage in agreement. Nevertheless there is considerable commentary that disagrees, particularly that which sides with Palamon in his victory and sees poetic justice in Arcite's loss.

40.   Cf. Donaldson, "The Ending of Chaucer's *Troilus,*" in *Early English and Norse Studies,* reprinted in Donaldson's *Speaking of Chaucer,* pp. 88–90.

41.   The exact meaning of Chaucer's words is not clear, but the association between Theseus and destiny is clear; see Jordan, p. 170.

42.   It is not odd for Chaucer to associate the heart with thinking. Notice the following passage on Arcite's death, and Robinson's note on it:

> And yet mooreover, for in his armes two
> The vital strengthe is lost and al ago.
> Oonly the intellect, withouten moore,

That dwelled in his herte syk and soore,
Gan faillen whan the herte felte deeth.

(I, 2801–5)

2803. The heart is represented as the seat of the intellect. This doctrine, taught by Empedocles, Aristotle, and others, was familiar but not undisputed. Galen, for example, assigned the rational faculty rather to the brain. (Robinson, *Works,* p. 682)

A trace of this rational sense of "heart" still survives in our expression for knowing something well and/or knowing it by memory: knowing it "by heart."

43. See Curry, *Chaucer and the Medieval Sciences,* pp. 144–48.

44. There is also a striking, though perhaps merely incidental, parallel between the speech's observations that

". . . therfore, of his wise purveiaunce
He hath so wel biset his ordinaunce,
That speces of thynges and progressiouns
Shullen enduren by successiouns,"

(I, 3011–14)

and Palamon's earlier supplication,

"And if so be my destynee be shapen
By eterne word to dyen in prisoun,
Of our lynage have some compassioun . . ."

(I, 1108–10)

45. Cf. Muscatine, *Chaucer and the French Tradition,* p. 190: Chaucer's "perception of the order beyond chaos."

46. Cf. Muscatine, p. 187: in Theseus' final speech, the "theme of love itself is submerged in the category of all earthly experience."

IV. 'THE NUN'S PRIEST'S TALE'

47. On Chaucer's polarity between authority and experi-

ence, see Robert Payne, *The Key of Remembrance* (New Haven, 1963), p. 63 and all of chapter II.

48. See Ernst Robert Curtius, *European Literature and the Latin Middle Ages* (New York, 1953), especially chapter VIII; and *Les Arts Poetiques du XIIe et du XIIIe Siécle,* ed. Edmund Faral (Paris, 1924), introduction.

49. ME *cherme* = the singing of birds.

50. Dante made a most intriguing mistake that bears on the relationship between language and gender. He argues in *De Vulgari Eloquentia* that just because Eve speaks before Adam in Genesis, it does not follow that women are linguistically prior or better. He argues with considerable heat. The odd thing is that *Adam* speaks first in Genesis. I cannot help concluding that even though Dante's conscious argument is *against* woman's priority, his more powerful act is to drown out his own knowledge of Genesis and imply that women *do* bear linguistic priority.

51. Pertelote even undermines the colors in her husband's dream. She says, in effect, "You think those colors refer to reality in the outside world, but actually they are just accidental fumes of what is in your stomach." His colored perceptions are only "derived phenomena." She does not, it is true, deny his *waking* perception of color — she does not go as far as Galileo and Locke in their separation of primary and secondary qualities. But the seeds of such thinking lie dormant in her tough-minded, reductive operationalism.

52. See E. Talbot Donaldson's commentary on *The Nun's Priest's Tale* in his *Chaucer's Poetry* (New York, 1958), pp. 942–43.

53. This ending is interestingly analogous to that of *Troilus,* which has also been accused of being piously tacked on. That ending says, in effect, "If only you take a

true view of this apparently sad and serious poem, you will see that it is funny"; while the Nun's Priest's ending says, "If only you take a true view of this apparently funny poem, this 'folye,' you will see that it is serious."

54. Payne shows how virtually all the early poems are structured around a dream or vision, a poetic narrative, a piece of personal experience, and something of an "old book," *i. e.,* ancient learning. And thus they all, to a certain degree, imply the problem of how to interpret and assess both texts and dreams or visions (Payne, p. 104).

55. For a discussion of *The Nun's Priest's Tale* as essentially about the human use of rhetoric, see Donaldson's commentary on the tale in his *Chaucer's Poetry* and his "Patristic Exegesis in the Criticism of Medieval Literature: The Opposition," in *Critical Approaches to Medieval Literature,* ed. Dorothy Bethuren (New York, 1960), reprinted in his *Speaking of Chaucer.*

56. See above, note 48.

V. FREEDOM AND NECESSITY IN CHAUCER

57. See also note 11 above. 1185; 1294–96 ("cage"); 1310 (life as prison); 1327–28; 2777–79, "now in his colde grave/ alone."

58. Albert C. Baugh, *Chaucer's Major Poetry* (New York, 1963), p. 377.

59. See Marcia Colish, *The Mirror of Language: A Study in the Medieval Theory of Knowledge* (New Haven, 1968), pp. 212–21, for the medieval practice of using human knowing as an analogy to throw light on the nature of God's knowing.

60. One of the most prominent oppositions or conflicts running through Chaucer's poetry is that between experience and authority. Obviously, it is yet another working

out of the problem of freedom and necessity. I refer the reader to Payne, *Key of Remembrance,* chapter III, for a good demonstration of how Chaucer ultimately affirms both experience and authority.

61. *Cf.* Donaldson, "The Ending of Chaucer's *Troilus,"* in *Early English and Norse Studies,* reprinted in Donaldson's *Speaking of Chaucer,* p. 95.

VI. IRONY RELINQUISHED

62. It is not a black-and-white matter. Irony may give a speaker or writer a greater *measure* of control, but ultimate control still remains with the audience for *all* utterance. Irony merely obscures slightly the basic feature of natural language. When I utter words, what I *mean* may be in my head, but what I *say* is something created by my audience inside their heads. In fact, my very ability to mean things inside my own head — my ability to use language — ultimately derives from past creations of meaning by my listeners. I learned to talk only because others were willing to listen and understand and respond. Once I had learned to talk, I could then, theoretically, learn to talk better by talking to myself; but, in fact, the main process usually involves meaning-making by listeners.

With irony it can *seem* as though I retain control not only over what I mean, but even over what I say. I can *seem* to reserve to myself the right to decide what my words really mean — and only when and if I choose. About any particular interpretation of my words I can say, "No, no, you do not understand, and that just shows you are guilty of exactly what I am satirizing. You are too blind to see the truth I have just implied." Ironic meaning seems to be less *in* the words, less *on* the page, than nonironic meaning. But in actual fact, ironic meaning is still in the words and on the page — in combination with the context — just as nonironic meaning is. It is just that the *way* ironic meaning inheres in the words and context is more subtle, more tricky, more subject to argument.

To summarize: with nonirony the speech community determines what the meaning is, using tacitly accepted, slowly shifting "rules" for interpreting words and contexts. Of course, there will be legitimate arguments over what that meaning is — arguments, in effect, over what these shifting tacit rules are and how to apply them. Moreover, there will be illegitimate objections from Humpty-Dumpty speakers who insist that their words mean whatever they want them to mean. But still, given that messiness, the speech community determines meaning. With irony too the speech community determines meaning, also using tacitly accepted, shifting rules for interpreting words and contexts, though there will likely be *more* legitimate argument about what the meaning is because the rules for irony are slightly trickier, and involve a greater dependence on context and sometimes a wider context. There is, therefore, more room for Humpty-Dumptyism. And so it happens that when someone actually uses subtle irony, listeners and readers may feel helpless: *either* because they slipped up on the trickier rules for irony and thereby accepted the surface meaning, missing the real one; *or* because they allowed themselves to be bamboozled by an ironist pretending to have absolute control over his meaning.

For a fuller description of language and meaning along these lines, see "The Doubting Game and the Believing Game — An Analysis of the Intellectual Enterprise," the appendix essay in my book *Writing Without Teachers* (New York, 1973).

VII. THE VALUE OF DIALECTIC

63. Ulrich Neisser, *Cognitive Psychology* (New York, 1967), p. 10. His book is a careful, conservative, and admirably clear account of the facts of perception.

64. Neisser, p. 120.

65. Neisser. See also Jerome Bruner, J. Goodnow, and G. A. Austin, *A Study of Thinking* (New York, 1956); Jerome Bruner, "Going Beyond the Information Given," in *The Cognitive Process,* ed. Robert J. Harper (Englewood Cliffs, 1964); Jerome Bruner, *Studies in Cognitive Growth* (New York, 1966).

66. It is interesting that a modern historian, William McNeill, who is not a Marxist, applies this model of contradiction as a superior source of fertility in history and culture:

> It was the Greco-Roman and Judaeo-Christian inheritances, however attenuated during the Dark Age, that provided the fundamental frame for the elaboration of high medieval and modern European civilization. This inheritance was shot through with contrariety. Europeans confronted unresolved and unresolvable tensions between the primacy of the territorial state as the "natural" unit of human society and the claim of the Church to govern human souls; tensions between faith and reason, each claiming to be the pre-eminent path to the truth; tensions between naturalism and metaphysical symbolism as the ideal of art. The barbarian ingredient of European tradition introduced still other contradictions — violence vs. the law, vernacular vs. Latin, nation vs. Christendom. Yet these polar antitheses were built into the very fundament of European society and have never been either escaped or permanently resolved.
>
> Quite possibly Western civilization incorporated into its structure a wider variety of incompatible elements than did any other civilization of the world; and the pro-

longed and restless growth of the West, repeatedly reject-
ing its own potentially "classical" formulations, may have
been related to the contrarieties built so deeply into its
structure. . . . In this, far more than in any particular intellectual, institutional, or technological expression that
western Europe has from time to time put on, lies the true
uniqueness of Western civilization. (*The Rise of the West*
[Chicago, 1963], p. 539)

67.   Though Plato's ontology seems peculiar to us, he was
clearly interested in this *kind* of thinking:

> Elsewhere in the late dialogues a similar account of dialec-
> tic is given. . . . In the *Politicus* the method is again de-
> scribed in similar terms: it is necessary "first to perceive
> the *community* existing between the many, and then not
> to desist before seeing in it all the *differences* that there
> are among the Forms; and then having seen the manifold
> *dissimilarities* in the groups of many, not to be put out of
> countenance or stop until, bringing all the common fea-
> tures within a single *likeness,* one encloses them in the
> essence of a "Form" (285ab). (Lloyd, *Polarity and Anal-
> ogy,* pp. 432–33)

68.   For an attempt to work out a detailed model of how
metaphorical thinking can lead to an idea that is genuinely
original, see my "Real Learning," *Journal of General Education,* July, 1971.

69.   J. L. Austin, *How to Do Things With Words* (New
York, 1965), pp. 138, 144.

70.   Austin, pp. 105, 109.

71.   Austin, p. 148.

72.   Charles Rycroft, "Causes and Meanings," in *Psycho-
analysis Observed,* ed. Charles Rycroft (London, 1966), p.
13.

73.   See Colin Turbayne, *The Myth of Metaphor* (New
Haven, 1962) for a discussion of the difficulties inherent
in our tendency always to link explanation with *cause,*

and for a proposal for using a *meaning* model instead.

74. Karl Popper, "What is Dialectic," in his *Conjectures and Refutations* (New York, 1962), p. 317.

75. Niels Bohr, *Atomic Physics and Human Knowledge* (New York, 1958).

76. Thomas Kuhn, *The Structure of Scientific Revolutions* (Chicago, 1962).

77. Popper's own theory of falsifiability surely sanctions actual situations in which scientists have to choose (for a time, at least) between two hypotheses when neither has been falsified — or what is probably more common, when *both* have been falsified in one respect or another.

78. Popper, p. 323.

79. *Forms of Intellectual and Ethical Development in the College Years,* by William G. Perry, Jr., and colleagues (New York, 1968) is a little known but very valuable study using a developmental model.

80. The *locus classicus* is Book XIII of Coleridge's *Biographia Literaria;* see also William K. Wimsatt, Jr., and Cleanth Brooks, *Literary Criticism* (New York, 1964), chapter XVIII.

81. Monroe Beardsley, *Aesthetics* (New York, 1958), chapter III.

82. Morse Peckham, *Man's Rage for Chaos* (New York, 1965). He overstates his case. Presumably art does other things too, from which some of its reward also springs.

83. We need more books that examine the structure of thinking of important thinkers by following closely their language, especially their figurative language. One such book is Stanley Edgar Hyman's *The Tangled Bank* (New York, 1962).